T.R. Briks

The Scripture Doctrine Of Creation

T.R. Briks

**The Scripture Doctrine Of Creation**

ISBN/EAN: 9783742862396

Manufactured in Europe, USA, Canada, Australia, Japa

Cover: Foto ©ninafisch / pixelio.de

Manufactured and distributed by brebook publishing software (www.brebook.com)

T.R. Briks

**The Scripture Doctrine Of Creation**

# CONTENTS.

|  | PAGE |
|---|---|
| INTRODUCTION | 1 |

### CHAPTER I.
On Religious Nihilism . . . . . . . 6

### CHAPTER II.
On Religious Nihilism (*continued*) . . . 25

### CHAPTER III.
The Alleged Law of Scientific Progress . . 50

### CHAPTER IV.
The Beginning . . . . . . . . 78

### CHAPTER V.
The Creation of Matter . . . . . . 106

### CHAPTER VI.
On Infinite Space . . . . . . . 128

### CHAPTER VII.
On Force, Law, and Necessity . . . . 143

## CHAPTER VIII.

On Creation and Life . . . . . . 175

## CHAPTER IX.

On Creation and Evolution . . . . . 188

## CHAPTER X.

Evolution as an Inductive Theory . . . 223

## CHAPTER XI.

On Creation by Law . . . . . . 243

Conclusion . . . . . . . 252

# THE SCRIPTURE DOCTRINE OF CREATION.

## INTRODUCTION.

THAT the glorious universe we see around us is the work of an Almighty Creator, the true and living God, is taught in the first sentence of the Bible, and affirmed throughout all the later books of Scripture. It holds the foremost place in the two main creeds of the Christian Church, and is there taught in the words, "I believe in One God, the Father Almighty, Maker of heaven and earth, and of all things visible and invisible." The Law, the Psalms, and the Prophets, abound in testimonies to this great truth. It is declared strongly and plainly in the Gospels and Epistles of the New Testament, and is proclaimed anew in the song of the heavenly elders, and in the oath of the mighty Angel, in that great prophecy which crowns and completes the written messages of God.

This truth is not set before us in the Bible

with nice definitions or metaphysical subtleties, which might only obscure its simple grandeur. But it plainly includes two main ideas, that there is a Self-existent Being, the Supreme and All-wise Creator; and that all other beings are creatures which receive their being as the gift of His bounty, and depend from the first on His good pleasure alone. Hence those weighty sentences of the Bible, "I AM THAT I AM... I AM hath sent me unto you." "Be sure that the LORD, He is God: it is He that hath made us, and not we ourselves." "I am the LORD, and there is no God beside Me." "I am God, and there is none else." To this Creator alone is ascribed supreme and essential goodness: "There is none good but one, that is, God." His nature, as revealed in the Bible, is inclusive of all good, and exclusive of all evil. He is Light, and in Him is no darkness at all. He cannot be tempted of evil, neither tempteth any man. He is "the Father of lights," from whom proceeds every good and every perfect gift. He is God almighty, everlasting, the Only Wise. He is Light, and He is Love.

This truth is the ground of all the morality of the Law, and of all the doctrines and promises of the Gospel. The holy will of God, the law of duty to His intelligent creatures, is summed up first in the Ten Commandments, and then condensed into two only; the first and chief of these being the love of God with all the heart and mind, and the second, like unto it, the love of our neighbour. Social morality, we are thus taught, is a reflection of that which has God for its immediate object. The lower duty is a test of the higher, for "he who loveth not his brother, whom he hath seen, how can he love God, whom he hath not seen?" But the higher duty is the source and fountain of the lower; for "the fear of the LORD is the beginning of wisdom," or of that moral goodness by which men depart from evil. So that, according to the voice of all Scripture, faith in the Creator, and love to His Name, is the only firm basis of social morals. A counterfeit, based on expediency alone, may do service in smooth and quiet times; but in times of conflict and temptation it is soon scorched, and, because it has no root, it withers away.

This fact of Creation, again, is the basis on which the higher doctrines of Christianity depend. Redemption is a new creation, described by figures and analogies drawn from this earlier work of God, which has gone before. Thus we are told that "if any man be in Christ, he is a new creature," and that Christians are "created in Christ Jesus unto good works." The whole work of mercy in the Gospel is described as preparing the way for a solemn voice from the Supreme Creator, "Behold, I make all things new!"

The discoveries of modern science unfold, in new aspects, the glory of this truth, which lies at the foundation of all religious faith. The telescope reveals the grandeur and vastness of the starry worlds, through illimitable depths of space. The microscope discovers marks of design and beauty, reaching down to objects too minute to be seen by the unassisted eye. But neither in the height nor the depth, in the vast or the minute, can physical science find any key to the mystery of life, or any secret that can banish faith, like a troublesome and useless spectre, from the universe. Multiplying tokens of design only multiply the proof that there is a Supreme Designer and Architect; and multiplying proofs of the reign of natural law confirm the presence and power of a Supreme Lawgiver. The accumulation of scientific facts has only a transient and accidental connection, in these latter times, with the growth of an atheistic school of scientific interpretation. Both are features of the last days, separately predicted in the Word of God. Increase of knowledge by the running of many to and fro is one sign of a moral daybreak that is soon to follow. But the unbelieving interpretation, or blind reliance on the constancy of natural laws, irrespective of the counsel of the Holy Lawgiver, is only one parting shadow of that moral darkness, which will soon flee away when the true Dayspring shall arise.

The object of the following pages is to examine two of those modern theories, by which the Scripture doctrine of Creation is wholly set aside, or else its moral features reversed or wholly obscured. The first is Religious Nihilism; or the view which maintains that the secret Cause of all things must remain completely and for ever unknown. The second is the theory of Development and Evolution, which denies any proper work of creation, and reduces all change to the operation of existing laws, of which the details may be explored, but the origin must remain for ever unknown. But the limits of the present work will allow only a few of the first steps to be taken here in so wide an inquiry.

## CHAPTER I.

### ON RELIGIOUS NIHILISM.

The Scripture doctrine of Creation is opposed in these days, not only by Pantheism and open Atheism, but by a rival which claims to be truer and wiser than any of these alternatives. This view may be styled Religious Nihilism. It affirms that Theism, or faith in an Almighty and All-wise Creator, Pantheism, and Atheism, are alike mere guesses in the dark, and that nothing is or can be known of that mysterious Something, which is the origin of the universe.

The Positive Philosophy of M. Comte includes among its main features this intensely negative doctrine. Every science is said to pass through three successive stages. Its unreasoning infancy is theological. It becomes metaphysical in its early youth, and dwells uselessly on abstract ideas of substance, force, quality, and causation. In its full manhood it puts away both metaphysics and theology as childish things, shadows where no certainty can be gained, and confines itself to the task of observing phenomena, and grouping them skilfully together. This view is said to result from the known progress and history of every part of science. But its main proof is sought in the many controversies of religious creeds and metaphysical theories, when compared with the rapid and steady growth of physical science.

The Positive Philosophy is thus an open foe to all religion, unless its newly-devised worship of "collective humanity" is to share in that sacred name. But it has found a seeming ally, on this main question, in a wholly different quarter. Sir W. Hamilton's "Philosophy of the Conditioned" is one of the latest forms which Scotch metaphysical inquiry has assumed. The acumen of the author, and his immense reading, have given his writings an European reputation. In contrast with French materialism and German idealism, he claims to give not only a truer exposition of the laws of thought, but one in harmony with Scripture, and with various testimonies of Christian divines. Its principles have been applied by an able disciple, whose recent loss the Church of England deplores, to repel the claim of those idealists who would dispense with all revelation, and pretend to frame a complete theology by *à priori* reasonings. Many have therefore hailed this new philosophy with triumph, as a powerful scientific ally to Christian truth. Others, however, have held that the new ally is a treacherous friend, and can pull down the presumption of a vainglorious idealism, only by involving all religious faith, natural or revealed, in one common ruin.

The First Principles of Mr. H. Spencer do much to confirm the truth of their warnings. For ability and original thought, this work holds an eminent place among English offshoots of the Positive Philosophy. Wholly negative in their religious aspect, his writings in other respects are constructive, and aim to build up a more perfect scheme of science on the ruins of Theology. Yet in these "First Principles" the maxims laid down in "The Philosophy of the Conditioned" are chosen as the best and most suitable foundation for that system of scepticism which is the substance of the whole work. However opposite to the aim of one, at least, of the two eminent authors thus enlisted in the service of Positivism, I believe this application to be logically sound; and that justice can scarcely be done to the present argument, until the stumbling-block involved in this celebrated theory of Sir W. Hamilton has been removed. Religious Nihilism will, therefore, be examined under these three heads—the Philosophy of the Conditioned, its development in the hands of Positivism, and its argument from the History and Progress of Physical Science.

### THE PHILOSOPHY OF THE CONDITIONED.

The doctrine taught under this novel and singular phrase may be given in the words of its learned author, in his famous article on Cousin's philosophy. A few words of explanation must be premised. Time, Space, and Degree are said to be three fundamental "conditions" of all human thinking. The Conditioned thus includes whatever is limited, local, or temporary. The Unconditioned denotes whatever is conceived to transcend and lie beyond these limits. The doctrine unfolds itself as follows:—

"Opinions with regard to the Unconditioned may be reduced to four. 1st. It is incognizable and inconceivable, its notions being only the negative of the Conditioned, which alone can be positively conceived or known. 2nd. It is not an object of knowledge, but its notion, as a regulative principle of the mind, is more than a negation of the Conditioned. 3rd. It is cognizable, but not conceivable, known by sinking into identity with the Absolute, but incomprehensible by consciousness and reflection. 4th. It is cognizable and conceivable, by consciousness and reflection, under relation, difference, and plurality." The first is Sir W. Hamilton's own view; the second that of Kant; the third of Schelling; and the fourth of Cousin. The first is explained by him as follows:—

"The mind can conceive and know only the conditionally limited. The unconditionally unlimited, or the Infinite, and the unconditionally limited, or the Absolute, cannot be positively construed to the mind. They can be conceived, only by thinking away the conditions under which thought itself is realized. Hence the notion of the Unconditioned is only negative, the negative of the conceivable. We can positively conceive neither an absolute whole, so great that we cannot conceive it to be part of a greater, nor an absolute part, so that it cannot be conceived as divisible; nor an infinite whole, nor infinite divisibility. The result is the same, whether the limitation apply to time, space, or degree. The unconditional negation or affirmation of limitation, in other words, the Infinite, and the Absolute proper, are equally inconceivable.

"The Conditioned is the mean between two extremes, exclusive of each other, neither of which *can we conceive as possible*, but of which, on the principle of contradiction and excluded middle, *one must be admitted as necessary*. Reason is thus shown to be weak, but not deceitful. The mind does not conceive two propositions, subversive of each other, as equally possible, but is unable to understand, as possible, either of two extremes, one of which, on the ground of their mutual repugnance, it is compelled to recognize as true. We are thus warned against recognizing the domain of our knowledge as coexisting with the horizon of our faith. By a wonderful revelation, in the very consciousness of our inability to conceive aught above the relative and finite, we are inspired with a belief in something unconditioned, beyond the sphere of all comprehensible reality.

"Though the Conditioned be one, what is opposed to it as the Unconditioned is plural. The unconditioned negative of limitation gives one unconditioned, the Infinite; and the unconditioned affirmation affords another, the Absolute. This agrees with the view that the

Unconditioned, in either phase, is inconceivable. . . . It is not a positive concept, and only combines the Absolute and the Infinite, in themselves contradictory, into a unity relative to us, of their common inconceivableness."

The application of this theory in "First Principles" to the sceptical argument, is made chiefly by a large quotation from the Bampton Lectures on the Limits of Religious Thought, and is given in these words:—

"The fallacy of the conclusions of Theism may be shown by exposing their mutual contradictions. Their exhibition cannot be done more clearly than by the Bampton Lecturer, whose words may perhaps carry more weight than my own, as written in defence of the current theology. . . Criticizing the essential conceptions in the different views, we find no one of them logically defensible. Atheism, Pantheism, and Theism, when rigorously analyzed, severally prove to be absolutely unthinkable. Instead of disclosing a fundamental verity in each, we seem rather to have shown that there is no fundamental truth in any. But to carry away this conclusion would be a fatal error. . . . . . . Speculators may disagree widely in their solutions of the problem, but they agree that there is a problem to be solved. Religions, opposed in their overt dogmas, are at one in their conviction that the existence of the world and all it contains is a mystery pressing ever for interpretation.

"Thus we come in sight of that we seek. . . . That this is the vital element in all religions, is proved by the fact that it is the element which survives every change, and grows more distinct the more highly the religion is developed. Other constituents of religious creeds, one by one, drop away; but this remains, and grows more manifest; and so it is shown to be the essential constituent. . . . If Religion and Science are to be reconciled, the basis must be the deepest and most certain of all facts—that the Power which the universe manifests to us is utterly inscrutable."

The conclusion here reached with such seeming pains and care, as the latest triumph of ripe and advancing philosophy, reminds one irresistibly of the Horatian saying,—The mountains are in labour, and a wretched mouse is born. This quintessence of a hundred creeds; this reconciliation of Religion with Modern Science, is found in the bare admission that the universe conceals some great mystery, "ever pressing for solution," but of which nothing can ever be known. A philosophy which deliberately prefers the search for truth to truth itself has its fit reward in "ever learning" under high pressure, and still learning only that on the subject of supreme importance nothing at all can be known. Again, a philosophy which throws a hundred creeds into its alembic, to distil away from the fermenting mixture every element of religious truth, is rewarded by the valuable *caput mortuum* which is left behind, total and absolute religious darkness. The words which Cowper's keen satire put into the lips of his "churchbred youth" eighty years ago—

"And differing judgments serve but to declare,
That truth lies somewhere, if we knew but where,"

are gravely reproduced as the latest and most precious discovery of advancing reason. It is strange indeed that a confession of total blindness as to the unseen and the eternal should be styled a reconciliation of all creeds with each other, and with modern science.

The Philosophy of the Conditioned may be examined, either as held by believers in Christianity, and honestly accepted for an ally of revealed religion; or else as held by sceptics, and made their lever to undermine and subvert both Natural and Revealed Theology. On the first alternative I shall write only in few words, and with reluctance, feeling that honesty of argument is most needful in defence of religious truth. It must always be a cause of grief and a source of weakness, when some earnest writers defend the faith by the use of premises which others hold sufficient for its overthrow. But I believe, for the following reasons, that Sir W. Hamilton's theory can be made to agree with the true sayings of the Bible only by such interpretations as amount to suicide, and extinguish all its distinctive features as a philosophical theory.

Christianity teaches that there is one True and Living God, whose wisdom is infinite, and "His greatness beyond our capacity and reach." But it teaches no less plainly that this God may be known, and ought to be known, with a knowledge as real as the knowledge of His works or of our fellow men, that ignorance of God is sin and misery, and to know Him aright the main purpose of all revelation. The testimonies to this fundamental truth, alike in the Old Testament and the New, are very numerous. [Comp. Ps. ix. 10, xxxvi. 9, xci. 14; Prov. ii. 1—5, ix. 10; Is. lii. 6, liv. 13; Jer. ix. 24; Dan. xi. 32; Hos. vi. 3, 6; Heb. ii. 14; Ps. lxxix. 6, xcv. 10; Jer. ix. 3, 6, x. 25; Isa. xix. 21, xl. 5, xlix. 26; Ez. vi. 14, vii. 4, 9, 27, xi. 10, 12, xii. 15,

xiii. 9, 14, 23; Hos. ii. 20, iv. 6, v. 4; Mat. xi. 27; John vi. 45, vii. 17, 28, viii. 31, 32, x. 14, xii. 46, xiv. 7, xv. 15, xvi. 3, 13—15, xvii. 26, xviii. 37; Acts xviii. 23; Rom. i. 19; 1 Cor. i. 25, ii. 7—9, 10, 12, 14—16, xiii. 2, 9, 12, xv. 34; 2 Cor. iii. 18, iv. 2, 6, x. 5; Gal. iv. 9; Eph. i. 9, 17, iii. 10, 18, iv. 13, v. 8; Phil. i. 9; Col. i. 9, 10, ii. 2, 3; 1 Tim. ii. 4; 2 Pet. i. 2; 1 John ii. 3, 8, iv. 6, v. 20, 21.] And the sum of their whole message is found in that grand saying of our Lord in His prayer of intercession, "This is life eternal, to know Thee, the only true God, and Jesus Christ whom Thou hast sent."

Now the Absolute and the Infinite, as defined and contrasted above, are no objects of sense or experience, since by the hypothesis these include the Conditioned alone. They are not names for the God of the Bible, who is and can be known, desires that His people should know Him, Hos. vi. 6, and treats ignorance of Himself as a grievous and dangerous sin, that brings down His judgment, Hos. iv. 1; John iii. 19; 2 Thess. i. 8. For by the same hypothesis they are "incognizable and inconceivable." Being names, then, neither of God nor of any creature, nor yet mere qualities, they must be metaphysical fictions, and fulfil the Apostle's definition of an idol, that it is "nothing in the world." Neither of such fictions, then, can be proved to exist, either under the law of contradictions or any other. The exclusion of both as false cannot be "subversive of the highest principles of intelligence," but rather the admission of either as true; that is, of an Absolute, which is only finite; or of an Infinite, really infinite, and still non-absolute, unfinished, and incomplete. Nay, if neither can be known or conceived at all, the acceptance of either as Ultimate and Highest must do violence to all Scripture, and would contradict a vital doctrine of the Christian faith.

It may be sought, however, to reconcile this philosophy with revealed religion in another way. The first principle retained may be the necessary existence of one alternative, the Absolute or the Infinite, and the second, their incompatibility. One of them, on this view, and one only, is a disguised name of the True and Only God, whom the Bible professes to reveal. Let this be the Absolute. The third maxim, that the Absolute is essentially incognizable, may still be thought reconcilable with the Scriptures, by assuming that the knowledge of which they speak is not real knowledge, but some kind of imperfect shadow. That it is not exhaustive and complete -the Bible plainly affirms, and all sober Christians allow. "We know in part." But that it is real knowledge, nay, the most real of all knowledge, since its object is the highest and noblest reality, the same Scriptures teach with equal plainness. Eternal life can never consist in a knowledge which is a fiction and a shadow. This difficulty the Philosophy of the Conditioned cannot overcome, without renouncing the faith, or committing suicide in another way. For if the Absolute has a necessary existence, and is thus a name and title of the Most High God, and still can neither be known or conceived at all, the sceptical conclusion is firm and sound. Theism becomes an unprovable hypothesis, and God, if He exists, is a Being of whom nothing whatever can be known.

Is it said that the Bible reveals, not what God is, but how He wills that we should think of Him? The assumption is fatal to the theory, no less than the simpler view which it sets aside. It requires us to know, first, that God has a will; next, that He is distinct from His creatures; thirdly, that He has moral preferences among the opinions of men; and fourthly, that He requires them to think of One, of whom they can really know nothing, in one especial way. If the Absolute be inconceivable and incognizable, each of these assumptions must be a blind guess in the dark, devoid of all real evidence. The view is not only fatal to the theory it is brought to relieve and sustain, but also casts a dark cloud over God's moral character. It ascribes to Him the desire that His creatures should accept a shadow of knowledge for a reality, because He is unable to give them any real revelation.

The instinct of dependence, and the sense of moral obligation, can have no regulative value, if the object to which they refer be wholly incognizable. For if we know that God is a Person, who has rightful claims over His creatures, distinct from them, Lord over them, the Supreme Lawgiver, whose laws bind them to obedience and reverence, such a Being cannot be altogether unknowable and unknown. In this case we could not be sure that each of these conclusions or impressions is not an uncertain guess, or even a delusive falsehood. It is impossible to obey One, of whom we do not know that He has given us any command, or to reverence One of whom we have no conception, and whose moral perfections, if such do exist at all, are completely and for ever hidden from our view.

The Philosophy of the Conditioned, in Mr. Spencer's First Principles, holds the foremost place in a supposed disproof and calmly philosophical extirpation of all religious truth. I agree with Dr. M'Cosh that this use of it is logically just, though far from the aim of its distinguished author; that it "prepares the way for a Nihilist philosophy," and "leaves no ground from which to repel the attacks of religious scepticism." If, however, we disclaim its aid as a treacherous friend, need we fear it as an open adversary? Are the fundamental conceptions of Natural Theology, as it affirms, really self-destructive? May the sceptic rightly infer, even from reasonings urged by friends of revealed religion, that "Theism, no less than Atheism and Pantheism, when rigorously analyzed, proves to be absolutely unthinkable"? Are strong and broad assertions of essential contradiction in all the main ideas of religious faith a safe and sure ground, on which to take our stand as advocates for the truth and authority of the Christian revelation?

The main doctrines of the theory are these. The Unconditioned is the genus of the Inconceivable, and the negative of the Conditioned, which last includes all that is finite, and alone can be positively conceived. This genus has two species, the Absolute and the Infinite, each of them inconceivable, and agreeing in that negative character alone. These are contrasts, and one excludes the other. They are two extremes of thought, and the whole world of the Conditioned lies between them. Neither of them can be conceived at all in any proper sense, but still they are contradictories, so that one or other must be conceived to be necessary.

These strange paradoxes, I believe, have their main source in two or three serious ambiguities in the use of terms. Knowledge, even when real, may either be partial and limited, or else exhaustive and complete. Conception may denote, either the power to form a clear logical statement and definition, whereby one object is truly differenced from others; or else the power to combine all these defining features into one complete and clear mental picture. There is also a true and a false Absolute, a true and a false Infinite. The true Absolute and the true Infinite are the same; distinct, but consistent and reconcilable perfections of the One True and Living God, the absolute and all-perfect I AM, whose wisdom and greatness are infinite. In the sense of limited but real knowledge, they may be known and conceived, and it is the sin and shame of every child of man, as all Scripture bears witness, if they remain unknown. In the sense of exhaustive knowledge they can neither be known nor conceived, since what is comprehended by a finite mind must be less, not greater, than the mind which comprehends and contains it. The false Absolute and the false Infinite, on the other hand, are contradictory, not only of each other, but of themselves. They are unreal images, in which the eyes of the soul see double; parhelia, occasioned by the light of the True Sun, but due to confusion in the mental eyesight; and are worthless substitutes for the true and proper vision of His divine glory. Instead of either of them, it is doubtful which, claiming justly a necessary existence, they both disappear of themselves when clear eyesight is restored. We then behold, though darkly as in a mirror, the True Absolute who is the True Infinite, "the Blessed and Only Potentate, whom no man hath seen nor can see" with perfect vision, "the King of kings, and Lord of lords."

These distinctions will enable us to judge correctly of the four alternatives in the passage quoted above. If the subject be the True Absolute and Infinite, and knowledge and conception are used in their second sense, for complete knowledge and a clear mental picture, the doctrine of Sir W. Hamilton will be true, and that which he opposes farthest from the truth. But using knowledge and conception in the more usual and practically the more important sense, the case is reversed. In this sense, the Absolute and the Infinite are cognizable and conceivable, as M. Cousin is said to affirm, by relation, difference, and plurality, and the rival doctrine will be farthest from the truth. If we speak of the false Absolute and Infinite, then in both senses they are "incognizable and inconceivable:" in one, because they profess to deal with an object higher than all those which can be contained or comprehended by a finite intelligence: in the other, because each is a mental idol with no answering reality, an artificial combination of imperfect notions; and the more closely these are sifted, the more plainly their self-contradiction will appear.

The paradoxes of the theory are as great and as various as those which it lays to the charge of Natural Theology. How can the Inconceivable be conceived at all as a logical genus, combining species of its own? How can contradictories, which exclude each other, be two species of one common genus? How can the Infinite, infinite not in some respects, but in all, be one of two species, and thus be doubly limited by a genus which includes it, and by a second species lying at its side? How can the Absolute, that which is "perfect, complete, total," be a species, and so a part, of a larger genus which comprehends it? How can we know the essential contradiction of two things or names, of whose meaning nothing whatever can be known? How can we know that they lie on opposite sides of the Conditioned, and that this forms a mean between them, as two extremes?

Again, if the Absolute contains all that is actual, evil included, and this and no other is the conception it requires, while the Conditioned includes all the actual universe, how can this Absolute possibly be an extreme, lying on one side of the Conditioned? If wholly inconceivable, how can one conception of it be required as more legitimate than another? If defined as the Perfect, why must the only lawful conception of it include all varieties of imperfection and evil? If an opposite extreme to the Infinite, and its contradictory, must it not be finite? If finite, must it not cease to be absolute, total, and complete? If the Infinite, again, is a contrast to the Absolute, must it not be partial and unfinished, and thereby cease to be infinite? If it rejects every kind of limit, how can we sever it from the Conditioned, as a mean, and from the Absolute, as a more remote extreme? How can the Absolute and the Infinite be alike wholly unconceivable, yet both be conceived as species of a common genus, as extremes with the whole actual universe between them, and again as two alternatives, of which one is necessary, and the other impossible? How can we compare four different theories on a subject wholly unthinkable, distinguish their truth or falsehood, affirm six or seven propositions concerning it as true, and reject twenty others as untrue and absurd? Yet all these paradoxes are directly involved in this theory of the Unconditioned. It can only trample on the alleged contradictions of Natural Theology by the help of greater contradictions of its own.

In the chapter on Ultimate Religious Ideas, in Mr. Spencer's First Principles, these *dicta* of Sir W. Hamilton, as expounded in the Bampton Lectures on the Limits of Religious Thought, are accepted for a decisive proof that all the usual arguments for Theism, as a reasonable faith, are self-contradictory and illusive. The only religious truth permitted to survive in the géneral massacre of creeds, is the meagre admission, that the universe is utterly inscrutable, and that of any Author or Origin of that universe nothing can ever be known. But this conclusion once reached, the ladder is thrown down. In a later chapter on the Relativity of Knowledge, a vital defect in the doctrine thus used for the extermination of all religion is clearly pointed out, while a powerful argument is offered for "the necessarily positive character of our consciousness of the Unconditioned." When all religious truth has been swept away into the vast, misty sea of the inscrutable, this palinode is the only way to rescue physical science itself from the wreck of all higher faith, since it is allowed that an equal mystery of seeming contradiction belongs also to the Ultimate Scientific Ideas. This mighty logical engine, having done its work of religious destruction, is suddenly reversed. By this double process Natural Science is enthroned mistress of all that is "knowable." To Religion, in the proposed reconciliation, is left the high privilege, as her sole dowry, of assuring us that we are not omniscient, and that some unknown thing or other must remain for ever wholly unknown! The later remarks, however, are just and true in themselves. They need only to be traced to their certain consequence, and they will enable us to reverse the destructive reasonings which have gone before, and to clear away the mist which has been thrown on the common foundations of all religion, natural or revealed.

The Absolute and the Infinite are not the same with absoluteness and infinity. Each name is twofold. The article holds the place of a substantive to the epithet that follows. It affirms some object of thought, differenced and contrasted by that epithet from all other such objects. The Absolute, then, by the force of the phrase, is first of all a definite object of human thought; and next, an object defined by freedom from various imperfections that belong to other objects. Thus the term itself implies a relation to human intelligence. To make the absoluteness exclude any such relation, turns the name itself into a self-contradiction, a chimera from the land of impossible dreams.

The Infinite, in like manner, is first of all a definite object of thought; and next, one which exceeds or excludes limits which our experience assigns to other objects. To define it purely by the negation of all limits, without any affirmation of some real, unlimited Being, contradicts the phrase, and robs it of all meaning. To infer that this Being cannot exclude or be differenced from limited beings around us, because this would be a kind of limitation, offends doubly against reason and common sense. It makes the absence of all limits to be the same with the inclusion of limits of every kind, in all the various objects that compose the universe. And it attempts to decide by a single vague and ambiguous term the highest of all inquiries, what species of limits are really inconsistent with the nature of an All-perfect Being.

The Absolute and the Infinite, again, are not conceptions purely negative. Rather, of all conceptions they are the most positive and real. Every finite, non-absolute person or thing combines two logical elements, real being affirmed, and the perception of some limit beyond which it does not or cannot go. Now BEING is a positive conception, but a limit, beyond which there is an absence of being, is negative. The Absolute, the Infinite, by virtue of the article, affirm BEING, and by the epithet set aside or exclude imperfection or limitation of being. The verbal form in one of them is negative, but in each alike the thought is positive in the highest degree. BEING is a positive idea, which it shares with the Conditioned. But there is the added notion of fulness and perfection of being, such as excludes not-being, limitation, and imperfection alone.

The contradictions ascribed to the Absolute arise from no genuine laws of human thought, but from faulty logic. Reality is left out of sight in an attempt to reason on mere terms, referred to something or other, said to be wholly unknown. But in striving to fix its nature, or prove its inconceivableness by abstract reasonings, we may err equally, whether we build castles in the air or throw down those built by others. The Absolute, from its name, cannot be so absolute as not to be even an object of thought, and so far to be in relation to him who thinks of it, and reasons upon it. The phrase implies some Being, of which or whom we think in some definite way. It is no species of the Unconditioned, for no genus can be made up of two contradictories, that exclude each other from real existence. It cannot be a contrast to the Infinite, unless the most perfect Being is clearly finite, and the Infinite an unfinished sum of parts, and no perfect whole. It cannot be unconscious, unless unconsciousness be higher and more perfect than conscious intelligence. It cannot be the same with the universe, unless a countless variety of imperfections, by mere accumulation, can make up Being absolutely perfect. The unreal images of those whose eyes see double coalesce in perfect vision, and reveal a real object, of which they were only the distorted effects. Just so the Absolute and the Infinite, when the mind is freed from its own faulty, illogical misconceptions, must meet and be combined in the same glorious reality, the great I AM, who made known His name to Moses, the True, Infinite, All-perfect, Absolute Being.

Freedom from imperfection, and absence of limitation, are ideas which plainly have more resemblance than contrast. They can never be proved contradictory, unless we can form a distinct conception of each, and of that reality in which they both meet together, or from which one only is excluded. All these conditions the theory itself denies. And thus we are led to a conclusion, in which the Manichean paradox it involves is wholly reversed and set aside. The true Absolute and the true Infinite, so far as they can be conceived at all, agree with each other, and also with the idea of necessary existence. The I AM, the necessary, self-existent Being, is truly absolute and infinite. But the false Absolute, which is only finite, and the false Infinite, which is partial and unfinished, agree neither with themselves nor each other, nor yet with the conception of necessary existence, and both alike are unreal and impossible.

That the Absolute and the Infinite are two alternatives, alike inconceivable, mutually exclusive and contradictory, and still that one of them, it is uncertain which, "must be admitted as necessary," is of all paradoxes the most strange and incredible. It is combined by its author with the assertion of "a wonderful revelation, inspiring us with the belief of something unconditioned, beyond the sphere of all comprehensible reality." It follows of course, from this view, that one or other of these names expresses that highest reality; or in other words, that it is a name of the Most High God, while the other must be only an unreal and impossible fiction. Thus we are landed in the strangest and most repulsive of all conclusions, that one of these two names must denote the True and Living God, the great and eternal Jehovah, and the other an impossible mental fiction; but that which of them refers to the God of glory, and which to the worthless fiction, is an unsolved mystery that can never be known.

To conclude, the Absolute and the Infinite, by the force of the terms, must denote some true object of human thought, some real Being, free from the imperfection and limitation which belong to every object of human thought besides. It is thus known by relation, namely, that of a great mysterious object of thought to the mind which thinks of it; by difference, as perfect Being, contrasted with multitudes that are imperfect; and by plurality, as more then all, distinct from all, and higher than all, those imperfect and finite beings. This Absolute Being cannot include all evil, sin, and imperfection, but excludes them. Their inclusion would destroy the conception, and substitute the non-absolute in its place. The Infinite, again, excludes real limitation, but not logical definition, since it is in itself a defining name. It does not require us to include all possible modes of being, since finite, limited modes are shut out by the definition. The denial to it, or exclusion from it, of every finite form is thus a logical, but no real limitation. For if the infinite in any way could become finite, it would be less, not greater than before. A ball is really limited by its own surface, and the space which lies beyond it. It is not really, though it is logically limited, when contrasted with its own shadow, or with the space it fills or seems to fill. The Absolute and the Infinite, as Being, may be known directly, like our own personal being, with a partial, but still a real knowledge. As absolute and infinite, they cannot be comprehended. But still they may be apprehended in their relation of contrast to the dependent, imperfect, and finite. The verbal negative represents an idea really positive, because the limit or imperfection set aside is really negative, though positive in its logical form.

A great and real mystery, no doubt, remains. But a like mystery, which transcends our knowledge, and baffles the pride of human reason, attaches equally to our own consciousness, and to those conceptions of matter, space, time, substance, motion, force, which enter into every axiom, postulate, or discovery, of physical science. In spite of the great mystery, which is undeniable, in these fundamental conceptions, men of science do not doubt the reality of their own discoveries, or the real progress which Natural Philosophy has made, almost in all its branches, in these latter days. There is just the same reason why Christian Divines, while they own freely the unsearchable mystery

D

of the Divine Nature, and that the God whom they adore "dwelleth in light which no man can approach unto," should still hold firmly that He can reveal Himself to His creatures; that He has so revealed Himself in His holy Word; that this revelation is one of genuine truth, and not of empty, unreal, uncertain shadows; and that concerning His nature, character, perfections, His works and ways, and His future purposes towards mankind, much can and ought to be known. For He has openly proclaimed that He desires knowledge of Himself far more than costly offerings, and the message has been given by the lips of His Only begotten Son:—"They that worship Him must worship Him in spirit and IN TRUTH, for the Father seeketh such to worship Him."

## CHAPTER II.

ON RELIGIOUS NIHILISM (*continued*).

THE doctrine that any true knowledge of God is impossible from the very laws and limits of human thought, is one main feature of "the Philosophy of the Unconditioned." But this dogma is further developed by writers of the positive school from their own point of view. In the First Principles of Mr. Spencer, and its chapter on Ultimate Religious Ideas, this principle of absolute religious Pyrrhonism or Nihilism is laid down with much deliberation, as the basis of a new system of scientific philosophy. Six pages contain the supposed disproof of the main foundation of Christianity, and indeed of all religious faith. But while four of these are a quotation, pressed into the service of a cause exactly opposite to the intention of its writer, the original part in this refutation of Theism reduces itself to two pages alone. The huge pyramid of unbelief rests on an apex so narrow as to be little more than a mathematical point. But remarks on which so vast a structure of unbelief is reared need to be examined on that ground alone.

Atheism, Pantheism, and Theism, it is first assumed, are three rival theories, of which the common claim is to solve the great problem of the universe. "The question, what is it, and whence does it come, suggests itself to every mind. Three answers, verbally intelligible, may be made, that it is self-existent, self-created, or created by external agency. Those are Atheism, Pantheism, and Theism. But none of them is even conceivable in the true sense of the word."

This first assumption is misleading, and untrue. To solve the great problem of the universe, so as to leave nothing unexplained, may perhaps have been the aim of a few self-conceited philosophers. But in the view of every modest and sincere Christian, such a claim would require omniscience, which is the prerogative of the world's Creator alone. Faith in God, in their view, is no skilful contrivance for solving all mysteries. It is simply the acceptance of a truth, which, when the eye of the soul is not blinded by sin and folly, reveals itself spontaneously, with less or greater clearness, to every reverent mind. They are not so senseless as to think for a moment that the great Creator, the Lord of the universe, is less mysterious, or more easy to comprehend, than the universe He has made. In enlarging their landscape, so as to embrace a higher and nobler truth, they are prepared to believe that the horizon will be enlarged also, and that the mysteries of God and the universe will be more and higher than those of the universe alone. As little do they allow that Atheism and Pantheism are two abstract rivals in the attempt to solve the same problem, with the least amount of mystery. They rather look upon them as vain efforts, under the influence of moral disease, to escape from the humbling and alarming truth of an account hereafter to be rendered to the great Moral Governor of the universe.

In the refutation of Atheism and Pantheism the only thing worthy of notice is a total misrepresentation of the Theistic argument. Christians condemn Atheism as unreasonable, not because it affirms self-existence somewhere, which they also affirm, and think it the height of unreason to deny, but because it ascribes it to mutable, limited, imperfect, multitudinous things, which have every conceivable sign of dependent and derived existence. The Theistic view is thus assailed.

"In the cosmogony long current among ourselves, it is assumed that the genesis of heaven and earth is affected somewhat after the way in which a workman shapes a piece of furniture. The assumption is made, not by theologians only, but by the immense majority of philosophers, past and present. But the conception is not even consistent with itself, and cannot be realized in thought, when all its assumptions are granted. The artisan does not make the iron, wood, or stone he uses, but merely fashions and combines them. The comparison does not help us to understand the source of the materials, and thus is worthless. The production of the matter out of nothing is the real mystery, which neither this simile nor any other helps us to conceive."

This misrepresents the usual view both of philosophers and divines. They do not overlook the contrast here affirmed, but, with very few exceptions, fully recognize it. They commonly distinguish between the first creation of matter, and the building up of the κόσμος, the whole orderly structure of the universe. The simile of the workman is applied to the second, not the first; and they connect it with the abundant signs of creative wisdom in the work of the Divine Artificer, and not with the mysterious act of power, by which matter was called into being. The objection owes its whole force to a careless error.

Theism is no vain attempt to solve all mysteries, and lies under no obligation to expound fully how the first creation was wrought. It rests on three simple truths; that Being does exist, that hence there must be self-existent Being; and that all beings around us, the objects of sense, and our own minds also, have no features of self-existence, but those of weakness, limitation, dependence, and continual change. They must, therefore, owe their derived existence to an Unseen, Self-existent, Being. The idea, so far, is definite and clearly intelligible. "By faith WE UNDERSTAND that the worlds were framed by the word of God." But still it is mysterious, and therefore we can understand it by faith alone.

The next argument is drawn from our conceptions of space. "The non-existence of space is absolutely inconceivable, and hence its creation is also. If creation were an adequate theory as to matter and mind, it must apply also to space. This must be made, as matter is made. But the impossibility of conceiving this is so plain that no one dares assert it."

This last assertion is disproved within a few pages, at the opening of the next chapter, by its own author. We are there told with truth that there are two views of space, as objective or subjective. The latter is one feature of Kant's philosophy, with whom space and time are only laws of the conscious mind. If so, plainly they must have been created along with these conscious minds to which they belong. The faith of all Christendom for ages is to be disproved by denying a notorious fact, reasoned upon, a few pages later, in the course of the same argument.

Creation, it is urged, must include the creation of space, and this is inconceivable and unthinkable. The assertion is trebly refuted by the admissions which follow. The creation of matter can never involve a creation of space, unless we are sure that space has a real, positive being. But we are told (p. 48) that space is unthinkable as an entity for two reasons, the absence of attributes, and our inability to conceive either the presence or absence of limitation. "We cannot conceive space and time as entities." Yet we are taught to reject the faith of the whole Church, and of the immense majority of philosophers as well as divines for two thousand years, on the basis of this impossible conception alone.

Next, the creation of space can be unthinkable only in some esoteric sense, since the whole argument requires us to think of it as either true or false, and one of the deepest thinkers of the last century has founded a school of philosophy on this very doctrine. Still further, if space itself be unthinkable, as we are presently told, why should we perplex our creed on the creation of matter by any appeal to an object of thought so unintelligible? If space be unthinkable, and existence without beginning unthinkable also (p. 48), then this alleged disproof of creation resolves itself into the certain clearness of a thought, the existence of which is affirmed, in the same context, to be doubly and trebly impossible.

The argument then proceeds. "To form a conception of self-existence is to form a conception of existence without beginning. But by no mental effort can we do this. To conceive of existence through infinite past time implies the conception of infinite past time, which is impossible."

The main reason for abolishing all religious faith, and denying the very being of God, resolves itself into these three sentences alone.

A miserable basis for so vast and fatal a structure of unbelief! It is owned, presently, that "it is impossible to avoid the assumption of self-existence somewhere." The proof of Nihilism is thus, briefly, that it is "vicious and unthinkable" to think of that any where, which, by irresistible necessity, we must perforce assume and think of somewhere. And further, that it is mere delusion, while we must assume self-existence somewhere or other, to deny it to objects plainly variable and imperfect, and to refer it to its only consistent subject, a pure, all-perfect source and fountainhead of created life and being.

In the rest of the argument, from causality and the nature of the universe, the parts are curiously reversed. The sceptic philosopher spends two pages in proving three Christian doctrines, as conclusions that "seem unavoidable." "We must inevitably commit ourselves to the hypothesis of a First Cause. . . Next, it is impossible to consider this First Cause as finite." Thirdly, "another inference is equally unavoidable, that it must be independent, complete, and total." The First Cause, it thus appears, must be infinite and absolute. These conclusions having been thus built up, the writer, instead of pulling them down himself, assures us that the task is easy, but would involve too severe a tax on our patience, and resigns the work to a Christian Divine, to prove that "the conception of the Absolute and the Infinite, from whatever side we look upon it, is encompassed with contradictions."

This application of the extracts from the Bampton Lectures reverses the practical end the Lecturer had in view. But the true reply is very simple. The doctrine may be encompassed by swarms of contradictions, as the Church is by armies of aliens, but it can never be proved to contain them. The difficulties thrown together, so as to cloud with doubt all the fundamental truths of all theology, may either be solved, one by one, by careful and patient thought, or at least be proved not insoluble. But to do this we must travel upward slowly, by patient induction, from plainer and simpler truths to the more obscure. And it may be safely denied that questions on the highest and most glorious of all realities, the great I AM, can be settled, either negatively or positively, by heaping up verbal contradictions, couched in variable and ambiguous general terms. We know and are sure, as Christians, that God is the First Cause, the Creator, absolute and infinite. But we know also that the absolute perfection we thus ascribe to Him as His due, does not exclude, but rather implies, manifold relations of authority, sovereignty, and active goodness, towards the works of His hands. And we know also that His infinity does not forbid, but even requires, that mental definition which contrasts Him with ten thousand times ten thousand creatures, and owns Him as Thrice Holy, the High and Lofty One, exalted above all blessing and praise. No view of His nature as the First Cause can be true, which sets aside or denies His essential fulness and perfection of being; nor again such a view of His perfection, as forbids His creation of a dependent universe. These truths, which a rash logic may call contradictory, are no real contradictions. We see them stand side by side, in sisterly union and fellowship, in that statement of the Apostle, that "He is before all things, and by Him all things consist."

The doctrine of Nihilism professes to hold an impartial position, and to prove alike of Atheism, Pantheism, and Theism, that they are unthinkable and inconceivable, and that of the origin and authorship of the universe nothing whatever can be known. But this neutrality is a mere delusion. Its own negative Atheism is just as complete as that positive Atheism which it disclaims and professes to disprove. For Theism is no abstract, unpractical theory of the universe. It is the belief in a First Cause, the Creator and Moral Governor of the universe, who has a claim on the reverence and love of all His intelligent creatures, and whom it is their highest duty to serve, honour, and obey. To affirm that there may be a God, and still that nothing can ever be known of Him, so that there can be no obligation on any other being to serve and obey Him, is to accept in words the existence of a Being, whose distinctive and defining character is absolutely and wholly denied. So far as the whole sphere of knowledge, life, duty, and practice extends, the creed is one of simple Atheism. It differs in theory, only by involving still deeper self-contradictions. However sad and dark, the view is morally consistent:—"I believe that the universe is self-created, and has no Divine Author, and therefore I own no debt of service to a Being who does not exist." But it is stranger still to say,—"I am not sure that there is a God, and I am not sure that there is no God. Of this only I am sure, that if He exists, I can know nothing about Him, and can owe Him no service, gratitude, or love. I am sure of this, that neither to love Him nor care for Him is scientific wisdom, and to love Him or seek to learn His will is a superstitious folly." Such a doctrine seems more unreasonable and offensive than even formal Atheism. Its wide acceptance in these days, under the plea of scientific insight, is a moral portent of a most unusual and startling kind.

The whole course of argument rests on the repeated assertion, that every belief on these great questions is "unthinkable." This new word, with which recent metaphysics have enriched our language, is a modern Atlas, condemned to bear on its shoulders a whole world of scientific irreligion. The self-existence of the universe, its self-creation, its creation by a Divine Author, the self-existence of the First Cause, infinite past time, space itself, its infinity, its limitation, its entity, its non-entity, the denial of self-existence every where, its admission any where, the objectivity of time and space, their subjectivity, the solidity of matter, its non-solidity, extended atoms, centres of force, the reality of motion, action at a distance, or by contact only, all in succession are proclaimed "unthinkable." Yet some kind of thought, and even laborious thought, on all these subjects, is seen in the very reasonings where this term is so freely used. These charges cover the whole range of Physical Science, no less than of Religious Faith. Their result, applied impartially, must reduce Science as well as Religion to this worthless truism, that the phenomena around us are indeed "a mystery ever pressing for interpretation," but that the impression or sensation of each passing moment is all that can ever possibly be known.

All these reasonings have no higher source than a mischievous ambiguity in these two words, unthinkable and inconceivable. Conceptions are either of the imagination or the understanding, and the latter may be comprehensive, or apprehensive only. Objects of thought may be conceived by the understanding, of which we can form no visual picture, or which are not conceivable by the mere imagination. Again, they may be inconceivable to the understanding in two opposite ways, by mystery or by contradiction. By mystery, when we recognize in them definite properties and relations, but feel clearly that in many other respects they are not comprehended, and are still unknown. By contradiction, when properties or conditions are verbally combined, and ascribed to one object, which more careful thought proves to be incapable of real combination. Inconceivableness of the first kind not only is consistent with real knowledge, but always attends it in a human, finite intelligence. The second kind excludes all real knowledge whatever, and proves that the supposed object of thought is misconceived, and that the union of characters ascribed to it is impossible and untrue.

Every where, both in Religion and Science, we find and may well be content to find, the inconceivableness of an ever-present mystery. From this the reasonings here opposed would infer what is wholly different, the unthinkableness of real and absolute self-contradiction. The difference of these two things is immense. The former is the condition which attends on all real but partial knowledge, and from which we could escape only by sharing the attribute of omniscience. The second belongs to the cases only where knowledge is impossible, and there is no consistent, real object to be known. God, Man, Nature, Mind, Matter, Force, Motion, Being, Self-existence, Beginning, all are mysterious. But if on this ground we call them unthinkable, and infer that nothing can be known concerning them, we introduce universal Pyrrhonism, and all religious faith and all physical science must perish under one and the same fatal blow. This modern giant of sceptical philosophy, in pulling down the strong pillars of the temple of knowledge, designs only to slay Religion and Metaphysics, that are seated on the roof above, gazing out on the blue firmament. But the ruin and desolation must have a wider range, if these reasonings have any real force; and will include all those disciples of physical science, who sit and feast, in fancied safety, without a glimpse of starlight, on the solid earthly floor of the darkened temple below.

## CHAPTER III.

### THE ALLEGED LAW OF SCIENTIFIC PROGRESS.

#### I.

ONE main argument in favour of Religious Nihilism, or the doctrine that Theology is a wholly barren and impossible science, is drawn from M. Comte's famous law of scientific progress. Every science, it is affirmed, tends to pass on to its full perfection by three stages, the Theological, the Metaphysical, and the Positive. In the first stage, natural phenomena are referred to deities, or supernatural powers; in the second to entities, or metaphysical abstractions, such as cause, force, substance, vital power. But, in the third and last stage; Science outgrows the swaddling clothes of metaphysics and theology, and confines itself to the classification of phenomena, and to that alone. It groups these together by a cautious induction, and thus detects laws of their recurrence, which may serve for the guidance of our daily life.

Such a law, when made the basis of a

scheme of philosophy, should rest either on a very wide collection of historical facts, or else on some proved necessity in the nature of human thought. But an induction, which should analyze the course of every science from the earliest ages, not only in its actual advance, but in the mental conceptions of its students, and the methods used in its discoveries, reducing the action of ten thousand minds, for thousands of years, on twenty different subjects, to one general law, is too wide and vast for any human mind to undertake with success. It is easy, however, to cast any number of facts into the mould of some preconceived idea. This is precisely what M. Comte has done. He starts with a ready-made theory, with which all the facts, by some means or other, must be made to agree. His alleged law is no result at all of careful inductions that have slowly led to it, but is a kind of metaphysical guess, invented at a bound.

The whole theory rests on three or four historical facts, the last of which refers to the special position and mental training of its author. First, there is the notorious fact that heathen superstitions of the most various kind, side by side with Jewish Monotheism, marked the ages before the Christian era, as far back as historical records extend. Since then, Christianity and Mahometanism, both Monotheistic, have been the creeds of those ruling races of mankind among whom science has been preserved or made progress. Next, a spirit of curious abstract speculation, derived from Greek philosophy, occupied the schoolmen of the middle ages; and, when science began to revive and make fresh advances, led to a great variety of abstract and metaphysical discussions. In the third place, after the Reformation, a powerful impulse was given to scientific inquiry; and Lord Bacon and others gave a clearer exposition, than had been given before, of that course of patient induction, by which alone Nature could be expected to yield her secrets largely to philosophical research. Last of all, there was an outburst in France, eighty years ago, of utter religious unbelief, in violent recoil from a corrupted religion, engendering entire social demoralization.

The founder of the Positive Philosophy spent his own childhood during the childhood of this infidel movement, and his youth during its youth; when, disappointed for a time in its political day dreams, it had returned with double zeal to the path of abstract speculation, and cherished hopes of new triumphs in days to come. Assuming Paris to be the intellectual metropolis of the world, and its school of unbelief after the first revolution to be the real vanguard of human progress, the materials for this famous law lay ready at hand. A metaphysical dogma on three inevitable stages of all science, invented by a solitary nursling of Voltairian unbelief, became the magic wand by which all metaphysics and theology were to be numbered with the nursery toys of mankind in ages of mental childhood, given up to oblivion, and done away for ever.

This alleged law must plainly refer to the methods used for scientific progress, and not to the favourite subjects of thought. It asserts that men, in the infancy of every science, seek its advance by religious ideas of some divine power; in its youth, by abstract ideas, such as force and causality; and in its full manhood, by rejecting both, and confining themselves to the registration of phenomena alone. Is this true? Or is it rather not only untrue, but impossible?

Now first, Theology, even in times of earnest religious faith, has seldom or never claimed to be an instrument for physical discovery. It has taught the duty of owning the control of some Divine Power in all physical changes, whether isolated and unforeseen, or within the range of human foresight. But it has not professed to supply the means for transferring them from the first class to the second, and thus enlarging the domain of science. If it has done this at all, it has been indirectly, as a moral stimulus to mental activity. For true Theology teaches that all the works of God are full of wisdom, worthy to be had in remembrance, and fully explored, and that not separate events alone, but the laws of nature, are from a Divine Author. Superstition, on the contrary, owning Divine power chiefly where no second cause can be traced, has often acted like an opiate, or played the part of a jealous rival, that fears to be a loser by every step in the advance of science.

The same is true of Metaphysics. Their abuse has tended to freeze science down into mere stagnation, while men have disguised their own ignorance under learned phrases and abstract terms, which taught nothing. But in their proper use they have only brought out into clearer relief those primary conceptions, or laws of human thought, without which observation can deal only with a phantasmagoria of perishing sensations. They have hindered physics by their abuse. But their use, within certain limits, is essential to the progress of science, and even to its existence.

And this leads us to a third fact, which convicts the alleged law of total falsehood. Men may doubtless study the laws of nature, and even social politics, and still shut their eyes resolutely against the presence and authority of the God of heaven. Modern Sociology founds its own claim to superior merit and wisdom, in no slight degree, on this fatal blindness. But even this new philosophy, with its most violent efforts, cannot get rid of so-called metaphysical ideas, or advance science a single step by dealing with mere phenomena alone. All its discussions turn on such topics as the indestructibility of matter, the continuity of motion, the persistence of force, the transformation and equivalence of forces, the rhythm of motion, the instability of the homogeneous. All these ideas or modes of thought are just as abstract and metaphysical as those it pretends to abjure. The main conceptions are those of the elder metaphysics, but under fresh disguises, or in new combinations.

This remark applies fully to M. Comte's own works. I open casually the first volume of his "System of Positive Politics," and in the first short paragraph of ten lines I find a crowd of metaphysical ideas and expressions (Système, vol. i. p. 110). Defining characteristics of systems of truth, the temporary and the eternal, the progress of doctrines, their final destruction, anarchy in the world of opinion and in the world of morals, implying by contrast rule and authority, the possible and the impossible, the contingent and the necessary, the strength and weakness of habits, freedom or compulsion in their progress, the essential and the non-essential in the circumstances of human life, ease and difficulty in mental changes, the pulling down of systems of thought by force, and their reconstruction, a true and a false future, the propping up of vain hopes by the aid of popular impulses, all are condensed into a few lines. No sentence of the school-men could be more densely charged, even to excess, with metaphysical ideas, than the first sentences taken, quite at hazard, from M. Comte's own works.

Astronomy is the one science, where we have a right to claim some evidence for this supposed law. Unlike Sociology and Biology, or even Chemistry, it is held to have reached already its positive stage. It began, we are told, with a superstitious astrology, which peopled the sun, moon, and stars, with separate divine powers, the heathen deities. In time these superstitions died out, and metaphysical abstractions, cycles, epicycles, and occult causes, came in their place, and retarded real progress. At length observation asserted its just claims. The Positive stage began, and its results are seen in wonderful and striking discoveries, the chief triumph of scientific research in modern times.

But this solitary instance of the grand law of progress, when viewed more closely, resolves itself into a great abuse of terms. It is true that an active system of idolatrous worship and faith coexisted, in Egypt and Chaldea, with the earliest recorded observations of the heavenly motions and changes, and the first stage of stellar astronomy. There was large room for the work of the imagination, where the subject was so grand and sublime, and so much remained unknown; and thus the skies were peopled with many distinct gods of heathen worship. But the course of those observations, by which the periodic risings and settings were ascertained, eclipses registered, and a period noted for their recurrence, was scarcely either helped or hindered by this idolatrous faith, which flourished by its side. It served as a stimulus, by giving a religious importance to the celestial changes, while, again, it might often deaden the instinct for tracing them to second causes. Clearly the Chaldean and Egyptian priests, the main supports of two main forms of heathen worship, were the parties to whose exact notice of the heavenly motions the first progress of the science is mainly due.

Hipparchus, the Greek astronomer, is the author of the next main advance in the science, and his careful observations enriched it with some important discoveries. He was probably as sincere a polytheist as other Greeks of those days; but since he came after Plato, Aristotle, Epicurus, Zeno, Chrysippus, the great founders of Grecian schools of philosophy, he may be referred by Positivism to the metaphysical stage. There is no proof, however, that either his polytheism or his Greek philosophy, to whatever school he belonged, had any marked influence on the course of observation which he pursued with such success, and by which the precession of the Equinoxes was brought to light. Clear geometrical conceptions, however, on the border-land of metaphysics, if not metaphysical, determined his practical sagacity as the foremost astronomer of ancient times.

In the modern stage of Astronomy, the time of its most conspicuous triumphs, the great Law of Positivism is not only a failure, but has been actually reversed. The Laws of Kepler were certainly a great step in advance; and these rested on conceptions of motion and geometrical figure, and numerical selection alone. Had Astronomy been content with these, and rejected all notions that lay beyond the phenomenal movements as worthless metaphysical abstractions, it might have remained nearly stationary to the present day. But when Newton once dealt with the conception of force, as the cause of motion, and used phenomena to decide, not the motions themselves, but the forces by which they were caused, Astronomy woke as from a trance at the entrance of this metaphysical element, and has moved on ever since, with great strides, towards its full perfection. Kepler's laws in themselves were empirical, and therefore sterile, however beautiful in their simplicity. Force, a metaphysical idea, needed to marry Phenomenal Science, and all the later fruitfulness of astronomical observation and research is due to this union alone.

Biology stands higher, and near the summit, in M. Comte's arrangement or hierarchy of the sciences. Does the Law of Eras suit better in this case? First, looking to the past, it seems impossible here to distinguish a theological and a metaphysical stage. As far as history gives light, the two conceptions have run on, side by side, that human life in all its features and changes is under the secret control of some divine power; and still that there are second causes, variously named as spirit, soul, mind, instinct, passion, appetite, vital principles, and vital force, on which the actions of living creatures immediately depend. The two ideas have flourished together for more than two thousand years. There never was a time so remote that the second conception was absent, and the first continues in full activity, as the faith of nineteen-twentieths of intelligent observers and students, down to the present day. The first, under the name of final causes, has even become one instrument in important discoveries, while the second has been involved inseparably with the constitution of this higher branch of science.

Have the Positive School succeeded in freeing the Science of Life from the infection of those abstract notions of cause and force, which they profess to exclude and abjure? Are they able to form even a definition of the science, in which this cloven foot of metaphysics shall not appear? Let us examine the definitions compared in Mr. Spencer's

Principles of Biology. Life, then, according to Richerand, is, 1st, "a collection of phenomena, which succeed each other during a limited time, in an organized body." This lies open to the fatal objection, besides many others, that it applies equally to the decay after death. According to De Blainville, it is, 2nd, "the twofold internal movement of composition and decomposition, at once general and continuous." This would include the action of a galvanic battery. According to M. Comte, 3rd, "the idea supposes that, not only of a being organized so as to bear the vital state, but also that, not less indispensable, of a certain collection of outward influences proper for its accomplishment. These two conditions are necessarily inseparable from the vital state, a determined organism, and a suitable medium." Again, Mr. Lewis defines it. 4th, "a series of definite and successive changes, both of structure and composition, which take place in an individual, without destroying its identity." Mr. Spencer himself defines it thus, 5th, "the definite combination of heterogeneous changes, both simultaneous and successive, in correspondence with external coexistences and sequences."

Now a series of changes may be the signs

and results of life, but are as plainly not the life from which they result. But the same definition (No. 4) further includes three metaphysical ideas, determination, individuality, and identity. If life were only a series of changes, what can the individual be, or what can form or constitute its identity? M. Comte's definition, again, is metaphysical almost in every word. It includes a vital state, which assumes the very thing to be defined, an ability to bear or receive this state, an organization fitted to this end, a being, that is, a cause distinct from the phenomena; organs or instruments by which this being acts, the vital state itself, its fundamental conditions, and their necessary and inseparable union.

Again, in the last definition, life is made to consist in the changes themselves, not in something which causes them. But then it is their combination, though what combines them, if life is only the changes themselves, is not explained. Thirdly, it is a definite combination. But how can their union be defined, except as common effects of some vital power? Fourthly, this combination must be " in correspondence with external coexistences and sequences." Here the ideas of being, of coexistence, of several beings, outness of objects distinct from the living being, and correspondence of changes without and within, which do not create each other, or a kind of pre-established harmony, are all introduced. Thus, six or seven metaphysical conceptions are combined, in the new attempt to get rid of metaphysics altogether. Biology, in the hands of the new philosophy, instead of life, vital force, vital principle, soul, or mind, may adopt a new and more complicated terminology; but it will be found to involve the old ideas in a new form, and to depend as much on the mysterious conception of something that lives and acts, as ever it did in earlier days.

Let us now come to the highest field of thought, Theology, which Positivism would set aside wholly as an impossible science, an effete superstition. Here, in Mr. Spencer's First Principles, and elsewhere, it has been sought to apply the same law of progress. After the usual unproved and unprovable postulate of Fetichism, as the earliest and once universal creed, a supposed historical argument is given, to confirm this theory of religious nescience, as the latest and ripest fruit of wise philosophy.

"The growth of a Monotheistic faith . . . is a further step in the same direction. However imperfectly this faith is at first realized, we yet see in altars to 'the unknown and unknowable God,' and in the worship of a God that cannot by any searching be found out, that there is a closer recognition of the inscrutableness of creation. Further developments of theology, ending in such assertions as that 'a God understood would be no God at all,' exhibit this recognition more distinctly, and it pervades all the cultivated theology of the present day. Thus, while other constituents of religious creeds one by one drop away, this remains, and grows even more manifest, and so is shown to be the essential constituent."

"Not only is the omnipresence of something which passes comprehension that most abstract belief,—which is common to all religions, becomes more distinct in proportion as they develope, and remains after their discordant elements have been mutually cancelled; but it is that belief which the most unsparing criticism of each makes ever clearer. The most inexorable logic shows it to be more profoundly true than any religion supposes. For this, setting out with the tacit assertion of a mystery, proceeds to give some solution, and so asserts that it is not a mystery passing human comprehension. But the analysis of every possible hypothesis proves not simply that no hypothesis is sufficient, but that no hypothesis is even thinkable. . . . The basis of reconciliation between Religion and Science must be the most certain of all facts, that the Power which the universe manifests to us is utterly inscrutable."

Here we have a strange specimen of that wide historical induction, on which some modern philosophers of the Positive School are content to ground their absolute negation of all religious faith. The pedestal here laid for the theory of Religious Nihilism consists of three sentences, all borrowed from one foot-note of Sir W. Hamilton's article on the Unconditioned; a text in the Book of Job, another from the Book of Acts, and half a sentence from Augustine. And the historical progress deduced is of the most amazing kind. Monotheism began, it is assumed, with an illusive claim to comprehend the One God thoroughly, and to solve the mystery of the universe without introducing a greater mystery still. At length, after long delay, as proved by the words of Zophar the Naamathite in the days of Moses, and by the altar of Athenian Polytheists "to the unknown God" in the days of St. Paul, it had developed into a truer faith; and the transformation into a confession of utter ignorance of the divine nature was completed by St. Augustine in the fifth century!

This alleged historical proof is, in fact, a condensation of historical falsehoods of the strangest kind. First, the date of Job is clearly before Moses, in the earliest days of which religious records, monotheistic or polytheistic, remain. Or conceding to the sceptic, for argument's sake, that the book is a mere literary fiction, still it must date as high as Solomon, and will be one of the earliest didactic utterances of Monotheistic faith. And here, in the words of Zophar, we find the doctrine of God's unsearchableness clearly taught; while, in the same context, a real, but partial, knowledge of God is no less plainly affirmed, and is put into the lips of the very same speaker. Thus the text, instead of proving that Monotheism ripened, after long ages, into a slow acknowledgment of God's unsearchableness, equivalent to the doctrine of Religious Nihilism, proves the exact reverse; that it began from the earliest record, with a full confession of that unsearchableness, along with as full an assertion that He could be and ought to be partly known; and it has never varied from this double testimony, for more than three thousand years, to the present day.

The second element in this historical induction is the Athenian inscription, ἀγνώστῳ θεῷ, with Sir W. Hamilton's translation, "to the unknown and unknowable God." An inscription on a solitary altar by Athenian Polytheists in the first century, or a little earlier, is made a proof of the gradual ripening of Monotheism towards the consummation of religious nescience! The version, again, of Sir W. Hamilton is disproved by the rest of the verse, Acts xvii. 23. If such had been the meaning of the inscription, instead of a suitable text for the Apostle's address, it would have been a decisive reason why he should have held his tongue, and abandoned his mission. The passage is a clear demonstration that, as Monotheism had begun fifteen centuries before, by the lips of Zophar, with affirming God's unsearchableness, so by the lips of St. Paul, almost in its latest Biblical stage, it renounced and condemned, with equal clearness, the creed of Religious Nihilism. The whole scope of his discourse at Athens is to show that ignorance of God was a sin, for which repentance was needed, and for which a solemn reckoning must be given before the judgment-seat of Christ.

The quotation from Augustine is no less

fatal to the doctrine it is brought to prove. The passage reads thus:—"We speak of God: how is it surprising, if you comprehend not? For if you comprehend, He is not God. . . . To apprehend God with the mind in some degree is great blessedness, but to comprehend Him altogether is impossible." Such is the clear, consistent teaching of Monotheism for more than three thousand years, from Job and Zophar, through David, Isaiah, and St. Paul, to Augustine, and onward to the present day. The three passages appealed to in "First Principles," to prove its progress and advance towards pure Nihilism, are alone a decisive refutation of this figment, convict it of totally reversing the truth, and scatter it to the winds.

That the doctrine of the Divine unsearchableness "remains and grows more manifest, and so is shown to be the only essential constituent" of all religion, is thus proved, by the scanty evidence alone brought in support of it, to be absolutely untrue. It is not one whit more manifest now than in the lips of Zophar, more than three thousand years ago; and its expression by modern Nihilists is poor and tame, compared with his early appeal to the consciences and hearts of men. Is it true, next, that the other constituents of religion "one by one drop away," and that their discordant elements are "mutually cancelled"? This also is wholly untrue. Christian believers, now, do not believe less than eighteen centuries ago, and their number is increased a hundred-fold. Some of them, doubtless, have loaded the common faith with various additions, disclaimed by others; and these discords have been turned by many into an excuse for rejecting the whole. The assumption in the above statement is of this kind. Successive generations of Christians have lived and died in the faith that they have known the true God, as revealed in His word, and that such and such doctrines form part of this knowledge, and are a sacred trust from heaven. A new generation arise, who reject this faith and disclaim this knowledge, who profess total ignorance of God, and claim this to be a proof of their superior wisdom. The fact may be accepted as a sufficient proof of their own ignorance of Him. Here, however, it is adduced as a self-evident proof that their fathers were wholly deceived. Is it then so certain that children must always be wiser than their parents? Is the old profession of Pharaoh, "I know not the Lord," the surest mark of ripening wisdom? Does it betoken eagles in philosophy, or moles and earthworms, to say, "Not only are we wholly in the dark as to any Power above man, but we are sure that nothing can be seen, and that all besides are in thick darkness like ourselves"?

Discordant opinions, whether in Science or Religion, are no proof whatever that all are equally false, and so mutually cancelled. This merely enthrones lazy ignorance as the best philosopher, and leads to universal Nihilism. The only just inference is that truth is not easy to attain, and cannot be reached by mere arithmetic and blind counting of votes, but by careful, patient, and reverent thought alone. And this avails not less in the pursuit of divine than of human knowledge; for God has promised, "The meek He will guide in judgment, and the meek He will teach His way."

The argument, then, in favour of Religious Nihilism, from two texts of Scripture, and a sentence of Augustine, combines every conceivable fault of reasoning. The evidence, if apposite, would be wholly insufficient in amount. The fullest assertion of God's unsearchableness comes first, not last in the series. The middle link is an inscription of Greek Polytheists; while the words of Zophar, of St. Paul, of Augustine, agree in combining the doctrine of God's unsearchableness with the great truth Nihilism seeks to abolish, that real knowledge of God is a privilege and a duty, and that entire ignorance of His name and character is a grievous calamity and a dangerous crime.

The claim is next advanced for Nihilism, that it holds this one surviving truth more clearly than others hold it. "The most inexorable logic shows" the omnipresence of something that passes comprehension "to be more profoundly true than any religion supposes. For every religion, setting out with the tacit assertion of a mystery, further proceeds to give some solution of it, and so asserts that it is not a mystery passing human comprehension."

This charge is wholly untrue. It virtually ascribes to all Theists the folly and profaneness of inventing for themselves the doctrine of a God merely as an intellectual picklock, whereby to solve all mysteries, and leave nothing unexplained. This is a strange calumny. No Christian believer is so foolish or so profane. They know well that, when a landscape is enlarged, its horizon is widened also; and that, if the universe is mysterious, its Maker, Lord, and Governor, is and must be more mysterious still. They do not expect to solve all mysteries in the present life, or to share God's own attribute of omniscience, even in the life to come. But they do not refuse to accept a plain truth, that there must be a great First Cause, a Self-Existent I AM, the Lord of the universe, when it results from all the facts around them, and their deepest moral instincts within; because higher mysteries, connected with His being, nature, and providence, are thus added to the deep and hidden wonders of the universe alone. They receive this foundation truth, as men of science receive secondary truths, on the ground of its direct evidence; not with the vain hope that it is a specific to solve all mysteries, and to invest them with omniscience, by leaving nothing unexplained and unknown. And they travel thankfully in the pathway of light, which leads them upwards to His throne; although conscious, at every step of their progress, that a blue sky of unsolved mysteries is still bending over them, that it attends them in their journey, and shuts them in continually on every side.

But the Positive Philosophy, though it begins with a doctrine of Nihilism, or absolute religious ignorance, leading to a practical extinction of all worship, because "the Power the universe manifests to us is utterly inscrutable," has not been able to persevere long in this pure negation alone. In the latest works of its founder he retraces his steps, and builds again, not exactly what he has sought to pull down, but at least a new Divinity, a new creed, and a new worship. In the "System of Positive Politics" we learn that "the grand conception of Humanity is to replace irrevocably that of God," that reason, joined with love, "alone completes the nature of the true Supreme Being, by revealing all the exterior and interior conditions of his real existence. Humanity has its objective dogma and its active aim. To this true Great Being, of which we are consciously the necessary members, henceforth will belong all the aspects of our existence, individual or collective, our contemplations to know him, our affections to love him, and our actions to serve him. And thus positivists, better than any theologians, can conceive life as a true worship." It becomes a true religion, alone complete and real, destined to prevail over all the imperfect, provisional schemes which have been derived from theology. "Real Science," that is Positivism, will have "a grandeur and consistency, never equalled, since it alone makes us know the nature and condition of the true

Great Being, whose complete worship ought to characterize all our existence." " No mystery can pollute the spontaneous evidence which is the character of the new Supreme Being. He cannot be worthily sung, loved, and served, except after a sufficient knowledge of the various natural laws which govern his existence, the most complex that we can contemplate. . . A last essential character, which belongs to him alone, must complete the fundamental conception, the necessary independence of his proper elements. . . The new Great Being does not suppose, like the former one, a purely subjective abstraction. For man, to speak properly, exists only in the too narrow brain of our metaphysicians. There is nothing, at the bottom, real but Humanity, though the complexity of its nature has hindered the notion hitherto from being reduced to system. . . Our Great Being is the most living of all known beings." (Système, vol. i. pp. 329—335.)

Here, then, as the culmination of the Positive Philosophy, which begins with Religious Nihilism, we have the discovery of a real Divinity, the only real being, who may be known and ought to be known, who may be worshipped and ought to be worshipped, and though no First Cause, is yet the Last Cause, or true final end of all thought, study, feeling, and action. Whether this new "Supreme Being," whose component members in that metropolis, where, as we were told by the same writer, the working classes formed the best prepared materials for the installation of this new worship, have been shooting down each other with rifles, cannon, and mitrailleuses, is less unthinkable and unknowable than the Holy One, whom we are charged to dismiss from our minds as a forgotten dream, may be a subject for grave doubt, even with these philosophers themselves. But at least these later views of the founder of Positivism furnish a practical disproof of Religious Nihilism, of a very strange and mournful, but of the most decisive, kind. The old saying is true once more. Those who refuse to retain the true God in their knowledge are soon given up to an undiscerning mind, until they worship a confederacy of human ungodliness, made up of Midianitish elements that devour each other, as more worthy of homage and reverence than the God whom Christian believers love and adore.

The New Testament has foretold long ago that, in the last times, abuse of the Gospel will prepare for a reign of selfishness, and a perilous and wide departure from the Christian faith. The rise and spread, then, in our days of a school of thought, which proclaims that the true God is unthinkable and unknowable, and that all religious doctrines are effete superstition, instead of proving, by the mere fact, its own superior wisdom, proves rather that this Divine warning is being fulfilled, and that times of great moral danger and religious darkness have set in. When a profession of total ignorance with regard to the Power which the universe manifests to us no longer awakens the cry of the patriarch—"O that I knew where I might find Him! that I might come even to His seat!" but is made the occasion for boastful claims of superior wisdom and mental progress, the signs of moral declension are complete. The descent below the standard even of the old patriarchs is mournful and extreme. If all mankind are prisoners of earth, left to grope in utter darkness, without one ray of light from within the veil which conceals that great Unknown Power, which the universe manifests, and on which all things depend, it is strange and sad indeed for men to hug their chains, and make a boast of their blindness. It were surely far better and nobler, like the Hebrew patriot in his fall, to long eagerly for the light which seems withheld for ever, and to mourn with him over our shame and misery,—

"O dark, dark, dark, amid the blaze of noon;
Irrevocably dark! total eclipse,
Without all hope of day!"

## CHAPTER IV.

#### THE BEGINNING.

"In the beginning God created the heavens and the earth." These words are the simple and sublime fountain-head of the mighty river of divine revelation. They claim, then, the deepest attention and the most careful study from every thoughtful Christian. In their original order they teach in succession four great truths, a beginning, an act of creation, a Divine Creator, and the reality of a created universe. And they exclude five speculative falsehoods; that nothing can be known of God or the origin of things; that there is nothing but uncreated matter; that there is no God distinct from His creatures; that creation is a series of acts without a beginning; and that there is no real universe; or more briefly, Nihilism, Materialism, Pantheism, Evolutionism, and Negative Idealism.

The Bible, it has often been stated, assumes the existence of God, and does not profess to prove it. But in this first verse a proof, such as alone befits the simplicity and grandeur of the truth, is really implied. The name of God comes third and not first in the message. It is through a beginning, and an act of creation, that we are taught to rise to the knowledge of the Great Creator. These two thoughts are a pathway that leads up to His eternal throne. There is a beginning, and therefore a Beginner, who " is before all things." There is an act of creation, and therefore a Creator, " by whom all things consist." The upward ascent is simple, but complete and sublime; and all later revelation unfolds consequences that flow from this fountain truth. They are all summed up in that song of praise of the heavenly elders—" Thou art worthy, O Lord, to receive honour, and glory, and power; for Thou hast created all things, and for Thy pleasure they are, and were created."

This first truth of the Bible, that there was a Beginning, disowned in sceptical philosophy, has not always been held clearly and firmly, even by Theists and Christian believers themselves. Those who strive to dispense, in their study of nature, with all reference to a Divine Power, find the process easier, when all the marks of design in the universe have been diluted and enfeebled by spreading them out over the countless ages of a past eternity. Each step of progress then becomes infinitesimal. Surely, they argue, the chaos of formless matter might raise itself slowly, by insensible steps, even into a universe of order, life, and beauty, when infinite time has been allowed for the progress, and every stage of the ascent is imperceptibly minute. If geology, for instance, is pleased to claim even trillions of years for its successive changes, what are these, when compared with the whole range of past eternity? That past time has no beginning, and is really infinite, is thus silently assumed.

The fact of a Beginning, however, as taught in the first word of all Scripture, and the error of the opposite view, of a real infinity of past time, seems capable of proof from reason alone. We distinctly conceive it impossible ever to reach the end of an eternity to come. Any future time must be only at a finite distance, however vast, from the present hour. Now it is just as impossible that the universe should have reached this present hour through a course of past, successive ages, really infinite. Past time must be finite, just for the same reason as the interval from the present moment to any actual future time. An infinite of past successive moments, already run out and exhausted, and the actual exhaustion of an infinity of future time from the present moment, are equal contradictions of reason. Somewhere, then, there must have been a beginning; or a mysterious transition from Absolute Being, above all time, and Absolute Eternity, out of all succession, to limited and finite being, existing in successive moments, such as was not once, and began to be. Time and the universe, it would thus appear, are twin-born, and arose together.

It has been urged, however, that the conception of a real limitation of past time, or of a real Beginning, is no less hard to accept, and no less incredible, than the opposite view, and that, in fact, these two contradictories, though it would seem that one of them must be true, are alike inconceivable. Thus Sir W. Hamilton says, "We are conscious to ourselves of nothing more clearly than that it would be equally possible to think without thought, as to construe to the mind an absolute commencement of time, or an absolute termination, or a beginning and an end, beyond which time is non-existent." (Disc. p. 28.) "Time survives, as the condition of the thought itself, in which we annihilate the universe." Similar statements are made by Dean Mansell (Metaph. p. 64) and Mr. H. Spencer (First Pr., pp. 47—49), and many others. "Time cannot be conceived as subject to any limitation." "We are totally unable to imagine bounds beyond which there is no space, and we labour under the like impotency with respect to time. It cannot be conceived to become non-existent, even were the mind to become non-existent."

If these assertions were true, and a Beginning totally inconceivable, it is surely strange that the affirmation of it, as applied to the whole universe, should be the very first word in that book, which Jews and Christians, for three thousand years, have received as a divine revelation, the true saying of God. It will be hardly less strange that one famous and wide-spread school of modern philosophy should have held that space and time are subjective forms of the thinking mind, so that their first beginning is not only conceivable, but a necessary consequence of the theory, unless we hold that these minds have had no beginning, and have thought on through infinite ages. This doctrine of Kant must be imperfectly conceivable, or it could not have been a tenet so strongly maintained and so widely received.

I believe it to be untrue, and therefore incapable of being properly and fully conceived as a reality. But the doctrine of a beginning is neither inconceivable nor untrue, but rather the foremost and earliest of all revealed truths.

The assertions in "First Principles" on this subject, when compared together, mutually cancel each other. We cannot, it is said, conceive of time, either objectively, as a non-entity, as an attribute, or as an entity; nor yet subjectively, as only a form and condition of thought. "We cannot assert of it either limitation or absence of limitation." The proper conclusion from such statements must be, that we cannot think of time at all, or form any judgment upon it of one kind or another. But when alternatives, one or other of which must be true, are pronounced in turn unthinkable and inconceivable, these terms must be used loosely and inexactly, with reference to one alternative at least; since one must be true, and free from real contradiction.

The phrase of Sir W. Hamilton, that "time survives, as the condition of the thought itself, in which we annihilate the universe" is plainly rhetorical, and inexact. We do not, and cannot, by our thought, annihilate the universe, any more than we can create it. We merely think of it as existing within a certain limit, and as not existing before it. We think, of course, in time, since we are a part of the real universe. We think of past time, along with a real universe, backward to some unknown limit, and beyond that limit we negative the existence of the universe, and of time also, as being a relation only among created things. Real time, of course, is the condition of our thinking at all. But it does not follow, either that we annihilate the universe, by accepting the truth that it began to be, or that the real time of our momentary thought proves the reality of infinite past ages, when no creature, thinking or senseless, had received any being.

Sir W. Hamilton appeals further to consciousness in proof of his statement. But my own consciousness, so far as I can analyze my thoughts at all, proves to me exactly the reverse. I cannot conceive to myself infinite past time as a reality, any more than I can conceive arriving at the farther limit of an unlimited future eternity. But if the entire absence of a beginning to past time is inconceivable, untrue, and impossible, then its existence is not only conceivable, but conceivable as a certain and necessary truth. The conception, no doubt, is linked inseparably with deep mystery, because it involves the recognition of a Beginner, above time, or that limited, changeable, successive, mode of being, which we experience ourselves, and recognize in all other creatures. But, though linked with mystery, the conception is definite, and results from a simple law of thought, of which the cogency seems irresistible, and cannot be shown to involve any contradiction. It is not only conceivable, but true; and not only true, but conceived, the more closely we reflect upon it, as a necessary truth.

The doctrine, for which the clearest evidence of consciousness is claimed, really consists of two elements, that time is a law of thought, not a law of things (Disc. p. 582), and that of this time no limitation or beginning is conceivable. Now this seems to combine together two things really inconceivable, that time is purely subjective, and that we are compelled to conceive of its existing without limit, wholly independent either of any thinking subject or of any real objective existence.

Time is a common condition of our own thoughts, our bodily motions, the thoughts of others, and their motions, of the state of every object around us, whether conscious or unconscious, and of the whole created universe. Thus it is objective, not subjective, or subjective only so far as the thinking subject is an object also. It is not a real entity, but a relation, discerned by thought, between successive states of all entities that are subject to change, and thus to all created existence. It is also conceived as necessary, their existence being assumed, and we cannot conceive of their existence, except as an existence in time. So long, then, as we conceive all, or some, or even one of them to exist, we are compelled to conceive the co-existence of time also. But we are plainly able to conceive one of them as having began to be; nay, every one, to which we do not assign a necessary existence. But if we are able to conceive the earliest time-limited thing we now know or think of as beginning to be, the further conception, that time also then began is easier and more natural than that of immense ages of time, with no changes of real existence to measure. The two extremes, that time is purely subjective, and that it is so objective as to be capable of existing by itself for ages without any thinking subject or time-conditioned object, are really inconceivable.

There is another source of illusion, on which the confident assertions just quoted seem in part to depend. If time were a real entity, no doubt we might conceive it as existing alone for ages before any further creation. But if it is either subjective only, or a relation as to sequence and change, common to all creatures, conscious or unconscious, thinking or devoid of thought, then the conception of a beginning of time must be possible, and will clearly involve no contradiction. How can a relation exist apart from things between which it is a relation? But it may still be urged that, wherever we place the beginning, at whatever distance, we can conceive of its being placed farther back. Does not this prove that the impression of an infinite past is spontaneous and irresistible?

A little careful thought will supply a full answer to this objection. Assuming that there was a beginning, and that its existence results necessarily from the fact of creation, and the nature of derived and dependent being, then time before this beginning must be impossible, and an essential contradiction. But since the actual distance of the present time from that beginning is finite, it follows that all shorter intervals have occurred, and that every greater interval is possible to occur, and will be realized in succession. Clearly then, if the true interval were revealed, we can imagine a greater, and thus appear in thought to push the origin farther back. But this is a mere illusion, because on this view, the Beginning is fixed in its own nature, but our Present is unfixed and movable. We are like the aeronaut, who sees the earth recede beneath him, when it is the balloon that rises, and the earth, in this respect, is at rest. Because our Present is not absolute, but movable, there is no interval, however great, at which we may not in imagination place other events, measuring upward. But this does not reverse the imperative necessity, in thought, for some beginning. It merely shows that we cannot tell, *a priori*, how far the universe may have already travelled from that origin along the course of time.

Past time, then, it seems demonstrable, is strictly finite in its very nature. The scoff of the young atheist, which represents the Almighty, in creation, as awaking from an eternity of idleness, has no other ground than a misconception of human fancy, a vain and illusive dream, as if ages of time could exist by themselves, independently of any created thing for time to measure. And we can never decide for ourselves, by mere guess, how long or how short is the real interval since this mighty universe began to be. Before the birth of our own race, and perhaps for many generations later, no direct human testimony is available. God's challenge to the patriarch must apply to every child of man in later ages: "Where wast thou, when I laid the foundation of the earth? . . . Knowest thou it, because thou wast then born, or because the number of thy days is great?"

We are thrown, then, for our knowledge upon superhuman testimony, or else can only form conjectural inferences from the facts which modern observation may reveal. But the only superhuman testimony is found in the first chapters of Genesis, assuming the Bible to be indeed a series of messages from God. The fact of a Beginning is here affirmed at the very outset, in full agreement with the voice of sound reason. But its period is not defined. That it was not less than six days before man's creation is plainly affirmed; but how much longer before is not at all, or at least not at all so plainly revealed. So far as the text is a guide, the separation of light from darkness, defining the first day, may have come almost countless ages after the absolute beginning of a created universe.

Let us inquire, next, what light can be

thrown on this question by just inference from the facts of modern science. The two sources of conjecture answer to the two words in this first verse, "the heavens and the earth." They must be either fossil geology, or stellar astronomy.

The first kind of evidence for past ages of time, before human testimony, is drawn from the strata and fossil remains of geology. These bear the marks of having once belonged to living creatures, and many or most of them to species which are no longer known to exist.

It will be plain, on reflection, that the evidence for long past ages, thus obtained, does not belong to the strict demonstrations of physical science, but is a presumption of Natural Theology alone. Once admit that there is a beginning, and a creation, and that the Creator is Almighty, and there is no past stage of the earth or the heavens, revealed by probable scientific inference, at which it does not seem possible, in the abstract, that Almighty Power might have called it into being. One form and arrangement of this vast, complex, mighty whole, would have been within the scope of Divine Omnipotence to ordain in the hour of creation, as well as another.

But when we turn from the attribute of

power to the higher perfections of wisdom and goodness, the case is greatly changed. We cannot conceive that the God of truth should have created our world as one vast magazine of deceptions, every where stored with illusive signs of life which never had existed, and races and generations of living things, which had no actual reality whatever. It is not less hard to conceive that the Living God, in His first work of creation, should store the earth with apparent signs of the ravages of death, and make it the facsimile of a vast charnel-house of perished life; as it came first from His hand, "when the morning stars sang together, and all the sons of God shouted for joy." We cannot believe that He would form dead skeletons, or their moulds in the strata of the earth, so as to produce a wholly false impression on the senses and understandings of those who might search out, in later times, the hidden works of God. The argument, then, for long successive ages of the earth's history, from the fossils of geology, is strong and almost irresistible. But it is really an argument from Natural Theology, and from that alone. Once attempt to turn it into a purely physical demonstration, and it wholly fails, or else needs to borrow atheistic premises, to make the reasoning complete.

The first step, then, in this presumptive evidence, throws back the beginning before a period of deposition of the earliest strata, wherein definite remains of life began to appear. A second inference is more uncertain. Experience illustrates the multiplying of individuals of the same species from one common stock. Both in vegetables and animals there is a natural law or cause, which can explain any increase of number in the same species, its higher origin being once assumed. When we have traced the world backward to the date of the earliest remains that have been discovered, we may accept the view that a further time is required for the increase of the individuals in the same species. But this conclusion is not equally sure with the last. We have no abstract right to assume that creation, in every species, followed the law revealed in the case of man, and was confined to the production of one pair alone. An opposite view seems more probable, that the number first called into being, in every case, would bear some relation to the place every species was designed to fill.

This presumption, then, from the remains of geology, carries back the date of creation to the deposition of the Azoic strata, but no farther. Science gives us no right to invent for ourselves races of still earlier date, which have completely perished, and of which no traces remain. No valid inference can be drawn, from such unproved assumptions, for the existence of vast ages of time, earlier still, which may possibly be mere dreams, and have had no real existence whatever. All conjectures that rest on the hypothesis of infinite past ages without any beginning, are wholly worthless, and are built on a foundation of sand.

The second class of presumptions are those drawn from stellar astronomy. The nebular hypothesis has had many disciples among thoughtful men of science. It supposes that suns and planets, our own included, may have been gradually condensed, in the course of long ages, from a kind of nebulous fire-mist. If the theory be true, it seems plain that an immense time must have elapsed even before the deposition of the palæozoic strata, where the earliest known signs of life begin to appear. Some have thought this hypothesis atheistic in its tendency, and even scientifically quite useless. Others, including many religious philosophers, think it highly probable, and quite consistent with genuine faith in a Divine Creator, though hardly capable of scientific proof.

Wherever life appears, the argument for

palæozoic ages has great force; since time is needed for the birth, growth, and decay of individuals, and for the coming in, to whatever cause we assign it, of new species themselves. But in the case of things without life, it seems at first as if all such reasoning must fail.

Let us suppose a vast universe, consisting of lifeless matter alone. Each atom out of trillions on trillions, has its own definite laws of force, with its own place, velocity, and motion. From these conditions their places and motions at any future time would certainly result; although, from the immense complexity of the problem, its solution might far surpass the powers of any finite intelligence. But from the very nature of such continuous laws, the series might be scientifically deduced backward as well as forward, by giving the symbol for time negative values in an equation of almost infinite complexity. Supposing the laws to have existed, a perfect intelligence might thus deduce their positions and their motions, for a million or trillion of years in the past, as well as for a million or trillion of years in the future. As a mere formula of science, the conclusion in either case would be equally certain. But then in the past it is subject to a condition, absent in the future, that time has really lasted so long, and that this universe, endowed with these complex forces and laws of change, was then already in being. For the beginning must be like a perfect mirror, reflecting the actual future in an imaginary past. It begins a long, unending vista of time and change, which it seems to bisect, but bisects in appearance only.

So far, then, this nebular hypothesis would seem to be wholly gratuitous. There must have been a creation and a beginning, however near, or however remote. But a creation of finished worlds, revolving round their central suns, is quite as intelligible as the creation of a diffused fire-mist, wisely and mysteriously endowed with such motions, positions, and laws for its embryon atoms, as to condense itself infallibly into suns, planets, and probable worlds in the slow course of immeasurable ages. And if equally intelligible, it is perhaps more attractive to the imagination of pious and reverent minds. How, then, can we explain the strong instinct by which many minds, not at all wanting in religious sentiment, have been strongly attracted towards some form of this nebular theory?

There is another remark, which may explain this secret, and supply a clear and weighty presumption in favour of this general view.

In the scheme of creation just supposed, two things would co-exist from the first, forces and motions. But these two ideas or facts do not stand on the same level. Force is a cause, motion is its effect. Force resembles life, and might even be called its lowest and most elementary form; as indeed the term, *vis viva*, enters into every mechanical theory. Thus it must be a simpler conception to look upon all motion as the result of forces bestowed at first on material atoms, rather than to suppose that one part only of the motion has this origin, and that the remainder was given directly by creative power along with the forces themselves. We should not count it natural, for instance, that bees should be created with all their marvellous instincts, and that, side by side with these some perfect hives of honey should have been created also. Motion leads us directly to the idea of some moving Force; and this Force leads upwards to the thought of a Supreme Power, to which all secondary powers and forces are due. It is thus no irreligious instinct, but a natural tendency of scientific thought, to trace back, if possible, the orderly revolutions of the heavenly bodies, to the operation of those laws of force, the existence of which has been proved and ascertained. This principle once assumed, even stellar astronomy, though it deals only with lifeless matter, may still throw some light on this grand problem of the first beginning.

Let us suppose, then, a material universe to be created, its atoms endued with attractive and repulsive forces, such as we know to be in operation, but very widely diffused, and perfectly at rest. By the action of these laws condensation would ensue, varying according to the varieties of that first arrangement, but still tending to the formation of distinct systems, with loose, outlying portions of mist floating between them; and, finally, of globes and rings, revolving in cycles of nearly regular motion, with unattached and less condensed nebulous masses subject to a similar process of change. It is conceivable, and not highly improbable, that the actual laws of force, if we could accurately trace their results backward, would resolve these condensed suns and planets into such a diffused, primitive nebula, or thin cloud of material atoms, and replace their regular orbital motions by a state of perfect rest. If this were so, and we then strove to trace the results of these laws still farther backward, it will be clear to any mathematician that we should merely reproduce their later states, with this one difference, that the motions would have an opposite sign, or a reverse direction. For the forces which generate any motion would plainly in the same time destroy an opposite motion. The abstract law, therefore, if time were boundless in the past as well as the future, would merely reveal two endless, infinite series of change and position, on each side of the state of rest. The one series would consist of motions which the forces are incessantly at work to destroy, and the other of opposite motions which the like forces are creating continually, beginning from a state of rest.

Now in contemplating a world of matter only, apart from all forms of life, the only real presumption for a distant beginning, instead of the creation of finished systems, consists in the higher simplicity of the view that forces alone were directly given by creation, and that all motion is the result of these forces; compared with the double process of imparting forces, and also giving various motions to particles or worlds, directly and supernaturally, from the Creator's hand. This presumption will plainly have double force against an hypothesis of motions being directly impressed, not to anticipate the results of forces implanted in creation, but simply to be destroyed, and be succeeded by a set of motions exactly their reverse, a state of rest of the whole universe lying midway between the two infinites. Taking the supposed state of rest for a limit, all that could go before would be only like a partial or total series of photographic negatives of all that would follow. Such a conception of the history of the material universe is unnatural and incredible. Our simplest view of a beginning, in the case of matter alone, is the existence of a world with innumerable forces, divinely given, but in which no motions, the result of those forces, have yet begun.

The nebular hypothesis, as a cosmical theory, rests secretly on the instinctive feeling, that the motions now observed are results, in past time, of those attractive and repulsive forces which still exist. The problem is far too vast to be solved with any approach to scientific accuracy. Still the laws of mechanics point clearly towards the conclusion, that the regular revolutions and rotations of the planets, and the nearly globular shape of the larger celestial bodies, would result in the course of ages from the known laws of attractive force, modified by cohesive forces, unknown in their precise nature, but which certainly exist, if these acted on a universe of matter irregularly diffused, and originally at rest. In tracing changes so far backward, we pass from effects to known and existing causes, from the more complex state to the more simple, from one where forces and motions their effects co-exist, to one marked by the presence of forces alone. But if we seek to travel back still farther, we only reproduce the very complexity, to escape from which we have ventured to travel so far; and introduce it anew with a fresh feature, which makes it doubly incredible, the exact reproduction of every later state of mingled forces and motions, only with an opposite sign, or a reverse direction of the motions themselves. And thus that deep instinct in favour of scientific simplicity, which forms the sole real evidence for the nebular hypothesis, and leads us to refer our revolving globes and systems to the action of created forces, rather than direct impulse from a Creator, points still more strongly to some absolute beginning, and forbids and excludes the hypothesis of a strictly unlimited past duration of the material universe. For this would be simply to invent, without evidence, and against all reason, a complicated series of unmeaning and worthless duplicates of all the successive states that follow an original condition of the universe, at perfect rest.

Astronomy deals with the motions of the heavenly bodies, and the laws of force by which these motions are produced or controlled. So long as it looked to their motions only, its progress was hesitating and slow, till in the discovery of the beautiful laws of Kepler it reached a kind of Pisgah, where a wider and nobler landscape began to unfold. But when once, in the hands of Newton, the idea of motion was made subordinate to that of moving force, the Jordan was crossed, the law of gravitation was discovered, and a series of scientific conquests began, which have never ceased to the present hour. The same instinct of science, mounting from effects to their causes, from motions to forces, the very instinct which Positivism seeks to annul and set aside, serves for a key, not only to the form and numerical relations of the planetary orbits, but to their sameness of direction, and near approach to identity of plane, and to the concentric and harmonious revolutions themselves. Why do the planets revolve in the same direction? Why do the planes of their orbits so nearly agree? Why do the moons and the satellites of Jupiter and Saturn conform so nearly to the same double law? How shall we account for the outlying cometary matter and meteoric currents more loosely connected with our system, for the revolutions of the double stars, and the aggregation of nebulæ, some of which offer signs of some process of gradual condensation? Science, in the presence of these great facts, obeys its own lawful instinct, when it seeks to resolve motions, however regular and constant, into results of the previous action of force; and thus goes farther and farther back in search of an origin, when this transformation of motions into attractive or repulsive force, their known and adequate cause, may be complete.

But the very same law of scientific thought forbids any attempt to go back still farther, when in the upward progress a state of rest has once been attained. It could then result only in exchanging the simple for the complex once more, and would replace by reversed motions, and an imaginary infinite past, like a dim reflected image, the successive changes of the real unlimited future. Here, then, when once in our ascent we have reached a state of forces only without motions, and of primitive rest, from which created forces might originate every later change, science must pause in her backward and upward progress, and resigning all that lies beyond into the hands of faith, must find a Sabbath after her labours, and worship and adore. "By faith we understand that the worlds were framed by the word of God, so that the things which are seen were not made of things which do appear." Astronomy rises, through the observance of the heavenly motions, to the conception of moving forces out of which all these motions may have arisen, and has discovered one at least of the actual laws of force, immense in its range, and wonderful in its simplicity. But the origin of the forces themselves can never be explained by any previous motions, or any series of material changes. They are gifts from the Almighty Creator, the work of His power and wisdom, and their existence resolves itself into the voice of divine revelation:—"In the beginning God created the heavens and the earth."

Geology, on the other hand, reveals to us countless remains of former life, buried deep in the strata of the earth. These appear certainly to imply long periods, when the plants and animals now entombed in the crust of our planet grew and lived under the influence of their own vital powers. As we go farther and farther back in the series, these remains vary plainly in their own character. They give no signs of recurring, stationary cycles, but of an upward progress, from lower to higher forms of life and being; or looking backward, of approach to a first beginning. The exact limit between palæozoic and azoic strata may be imperfectly defined, and need to be corrected from time to time by further discoveries; but the general nature of the series results from a large and wide induction, which it violates every law of science to reverse or annul by mere guesses without evidence. The higher forms of life succeed the lower, and the highest of all, Man, is the latest also; while traces even of the lower forms, as we ascend in time, or descend in geological position, become faint and low, and seem ready to disappear. Force is like the lowest form of life, and the life even of the spawn or animalcule is a higher kind of force than indiscriminate attraction and repulsion alone. Science, then, here also, when astronomy is compared, points to a succession of beginnings; first of force alone, without which there is no matter, the earliest and lowest gift of the Creator in our visible world; then life in higher and higher forms, successively later and later in their birth. But when, in each case, we reach the beginning, physical science has exhausted its powers, and must resign all beyond into the hand of faith, or that higher science which unfolds the certain being of the great First Cause of all, the attributes and perfections of the true and living God. Before the great mystery of life, half-believers and unbelievers themselves being witness, the pride of science must stand abashed, its eager curiosity turns into awe-struck silence. When it has reached these mountain-tops, it finds the vast blue heaven still bending over it. What can it do, what ought it to do, but kneel down with reverence, and humbly adore? Force is the gift of some Power which is Almighty, and life bears witness to the creative power of the Living God. With Him, and with Him alone, is the fountain of life, in all its wonderful and most varied forms, from the insect that sports its little day in the sunbeam, through all living creatures here below, to Man, the highest in this visible world; and higher still, to the seraphs who veil their glorious faces with wings of light, while they worship the Thrice Holy before His eternal throne.

# CHAPTER V.

### THE CREATION OF MATTER.

The Bible, in its very first word, affirms a beginning. Science also, when closely examined, points not obscurely to the same truth. Both exclude, as a mere figment, the idea of a succession of past ages of time, strictly infinite, a view which strives to escape from a divine mystery, only to involve us in a direct contradiction of sound reason. But the second word of the same message affirms an act of divine power, by which the universe came first into being. This assertion may be viewed separately, as it refers to lifeless matter, or to all the forms of life, ascending from the lowest to the highest. In each aspect it is opposed to the Materialism, which claims the self-existence for matter, by faith ascribed to God only; and to the Nihilism, which denies that of God and creation any thing whatever can be known.

The doctrine of Scripture is plain. Matter was created, and began to be. Its existence is due to the will and fiat of the Creator, the

I AM, the self-existent and all-perfect being. "All things were made by Him, and without Him was not any one thing made, that is made." "He spake, and it was done," and "by Him all things consist." The course of reasoning also is brief and plain. We are conscious of our own existence, and know also, by perception, the existence of things around us, and of a material world. Endless backward derivation is impossible, and hence self-existence somewhere, of some being or other, there must be. But we are conscious in ourselves of change, limitation, dependence, and weakness, and discern these same characters in our fellow-men. Lifeless, unconscious matter, we see plainly, is even lower and more passive than ourselves. We cannot then associate with either class of objects, or with ourselves, the idea of self-existence. There must thus be some Being, higher than man, free from the dependence and weakness of which we are conscious, the Self-existent, the Source of all dependent beings which had their birth in time, and began to be.

Materialism, in its naked form, hardly deserves a formal refutation. Heathen Polytheism, with its gods many and lords many, was far less unreasonable. Its deities were at least assumed to be limited in number, higher than man in dignity, and thus nearer to the Fountain of being. But lifeless matter is below man in dignity, and not above him. It is passive, dependent, unconscious, multitudinous. Thus, of all objects of human thought, it is most remote from the idea of self-existence. All modern discovery has increased or unfolded, and not lessened, this fundamental contrast. The telescope, on the one hand, and the microscope on the other, have greatly enlarged our view of the vast and countless multiplicity of material atoms. Physical astronomy reduces the suns and planets to globes of matter, resembling that of the earth, containing known chemical elements, and subject to the laws of material change. Whether, then, we assume all these trillions or decillions of atoms to be, one by one, self-existent, and truly divine, or that some of them only are divine, and have given birth to the rest, the hypothesis appears too senseless to be received even by the most rash and brutish of irreligious men. It would mitigate, not aggravate its character, if we were to style it a maggot theory of the universe. For even the lowest forms of life, bred out of the dissolution of the higher and nobler, are still higher than unconscious Matter in the scale of being.

Chaos can never be the One Self-existent, the true and sole Divinity.

Materialism, then, in these days has usually recourse to Nihilism, to conceal a little its own shame. God may perhaps be only Matter, and Matter may perhaps be the only God, if the true nature of God and of Matter is equally inscrutable, and veiled from us for ever in total darkness. It may then be affirmed that this alternative is equally possible, equally probable, with the Christian faith, and that it can be no duty of ours, when left in total darkness, to choose between them. If the Power which the universe manifests be "utterly inscrutable," then it may be trillions of atoms of hydrogen, with as many of oxygen, or an ocean filled with jelly-fishes, or an ape or monkey, or a race of monkeys, or a first man, or a race of men, or the God whom the Bible professes to reveal. But, in the thick darkness to which the new philosophy condemns us, all these alternatives are equally possible, and the truth remains wholly and for ever unknown.

Now the argument for Theism does not require a full and perfect conception, either of the great Creator, or of the constitution of matter. It rests on two simple premises, that " it is impossible to avoid making the assumption of self-existence somewhere," and that this conception wholly disagrees with the known characters of material atoms, their almost inconceivable number, their minuteness, unconsciousness, passiveness, and dependence. But since the attempt is made, in these days, to build a theory of Religious Nihilism or utter nescience, on a pedestal made up of unsolved mysteries, and fancied contradictions, it may be well to inquire whether some, at least, of the clouds thus raised to obscure our vision, may not, by patient thought, be cleared away. The remarks on the Unknowable in "First Principles," chap. ii.—v., are a convenient basis for such a brief review.

The Nihilist Theory, which Mr. Spencer shares with the disciples of Positivism, while disclaiming M. Comte's theories on many important questions of philosophy, as presented in these chapters, has one fatal defect. By proving too much it proves nothing, and betrays its own inherent falsehood. It abolishes all possible theology by abolishing equally all possible science. The reasons, from which it infers that nothing at all can be known of God, have precisely the same efficacy to prove that nothing can be known of any object of thought whatever. The Ultimate Religious Ideas, and the

Ultimate Scientific Ideas, are pronounced alike to be "unthinkable and inconceivable." The only just conclusion from such premises must be, either that knowledge is possible both in Religion and Physical Science, or in neither. But the legs of the lame are not equal. The conclusion actually drawn is that all Theology beyond the admission that there is a mysterious Something of which nothing can be known, is a fiction; but that Science may claim a wide, progressive, and ever enlarging domain of ascertained and ascertainable truth. How shall we account, unless by some strange and fatal moral bias, for premises exactly similar in the two cases leading thus to wholly opposite conclusions?

The same inference is drawn from another kindred principle, the relativity of all knowledge. The phrase is ambiguous. But whatever its precise meaning, still, by the hypothesis, our knowledge of chemical elements, of suns and planets, of animals and men, is no less relative than our knowledge of the Creator. Why, then, may we not be able to learn things of the highest importance concerning the God who made us, as well as to discover many things of practical use and moment concerning the works He has made? Since all knowledge alike is relative, why should we be zealous and diligent students in all its lower branches, which relate to things beneath us, and be careless idlers, or flippant unbelievers, with regard to a far nobler subject, the knowledge of our Creator, and find excuses for resting content with ignorance in that one subject alone?

Real difficulties, and even apparent contradictions, in our popular conceptions of matter, space, time, motion, and force, are counted no disproof of the claim of geometry, mechanics, chemistry, and astronomy, into which these conceptions enter throughout, to be real and progressive sciences, where much has been learned already, and further discoveries will be made. The like difficulties or mysteries in our conceptions of the First Cause, the Absolute, and the Infinite, can thus be no disproof of a real, and even a progressive, science of Theology. The contrast is less intellectual than moral. Most men take pleasure in enlarging their knowledge of nature, and their own ability to predict or control physical changes. But too many, alas! dislike to draw near their Creator, or to deepen their sense of His supreme authority and moral dominion. They fulfil too often, and sometimes are hardly aware of it themselves, the sorrowful description of the Patriarch:—"Which say unto the Almighty, 'Depart from us, for we desire not the knowledge of Thy ways.'"

This Nihilist argument rests mainly on the misuse of ambiguous terms, and a most deceptive antithesis between Science and Religion.

The three main subjects of human thought, the objects of actual or possible science, are Nature, Man, and God. The answering categories of thought are Physics or Natural Philosophy, Humanity, and Theology. In each there is, or may be, something that is known; and there is also, and must be, unless we were omniscient, much that is still unknown. The first constitutes science, the second its attendant mystery. Thus there is a Natural Science, and there are Physical Mysteries; there is Human, that is, Biological, Social, and Moral Science, and there are Human Mysteries; there is a Theological Science, and there are Divine Mysteries. The higher we rise in the scale of being, from things beneath us to the God above us, the larger the proportion of the Unknown to the Known is likely to be.

Science, however, is sometimes taken in a limited sense for Physical Science alone. The Positive Philosophy, and Mr. Spencer also, though less its disciple than a collateral ally,

I

extend the title to include Human or Social Science also. Next, because the highest subject is the most mysterious, Religion is made an equivalent for pure mystery. By this double, silent process, Theology is shut out entirely from the domain of Science, Religion sinks into a synonym for nescience; and Science is condemned to grind in a prison-house of utter irreligion, without one ray of heavenly light being allowed to disturb the settled midnight gloom. This strange fallacy leads to such statements as these.

"Religion has from the first struggled to unite more or less science with its nescience. Science has from the first kept hold of more or less nescience, as a part of science. Each has been obliged gradually to relinquish that which it had wrongly claimed, while it has gained from the other that to which it had the right. Religion has been compelled by Science to give up one and another of its dogmas. Partly through the criticisms of Religion, Science has been compelled to abandon attempts to include within the bounds of knowledge that which cannot be known."

The confusion of thought, in this proposed basis of the Sceptical Philosophy, is complete and entire. First, Religion is properly a name for sentiment, duty, moral obligation, and not for knowledge, whether real or fancied only; and its proper antithesis is the ardour of M. Comte and his thorough disciples in the worship of Humanity, their new Supreme Being. There is one contrast, in the subject of knowledge, between Theology on one side, and Humanity and Physics on the other. There is a second contrast, wholly distinct, in the degrees of knowledge or ignorance possible or conceivable, science being the mean, and nescience and omniscience the two extremes. And thus an antithesis of Theology and Science, when laid as the basis of a school of philosophy, is a pure and simple delusion. Physics and Humanity have their mysteries, no less than Theology; deep, unsolved, inscrutable without Omniscience. Theology has its science, real, firm, progressive, no less than Physics and Humanity. Only this nobler science, "the knowledge of the holy" (Prov. ix. 10; xxx. 3) is harder of attainment, and has stricter and more rigid moral conditions. It is secured by God's own promise to humble and reverent hearts, and to these alone.

If Science is to denote knowledge in contrast to mystery, how can ultimate scientific ideas, like ultimate religious ideas, be "unthinkable and inconceivable"? This fact alone would then prove them to be religious, not scientific. Again, if the definition of Religion be mystery or nescience, it is waste of time to spend pages in proving that no religious truth can be known. The whole course of reasoning vanishes into thin air, when once the true contrast is restored. Theology has its deep, unsolved mysteries, but Physics have the same. Our conceptions of matter, divisibility, force, motion, space, time, solidity, involve, on a hasty view, many seeming contradictions, no less than those of the First Cause, the Absolute, the Infinite, the Eternal. The true conclusion, then, exactly reverses the one actually drawn. In spite of the mystery in Ultimate Physical Ideas, there may be and is a true and progressive Physical Science. So, too, in spite of mystery in the Ultimate Religious Ideas, there may be, and blessed be God, there is, a true, real, progressive Theological Science.

The Creation of Matter must plainly involve a twofold mystery, one depending on our ignorance of the nature of Matter, the other, of the nature and being of God. The Ultimate Ideas, on each side, have been alleged to be unthinkable. Religious Nihilism, then, to be consistent, ought to include Physical Nihilism, so that Theology and Physics might expire peacefully together in each other's arms. To avoid this, the only logical conclusion from the theory, an exchange is made. All the mysteries of Physics are charitably made over to Theology, to enlarge the range of its valuable monopoly of total nescience, and to compensate for the sacrilege, which would rob it of the possession of one single grain of known and certain truth. But all mystery is not contradiction; and perhaps, when a little more light has been gained, the mysteries in these two extremes of thought, the Living God, and lifeless, insentient matter, may even throw some partial light upon each other. That view of the constitution of matter, to which, as I believe, the advance of modern science is surely leading us, though not essential to the Theistic argument, which is simpler in its basis, adds to it new cogency, and places it in a clearer light. And no wonder; for Nihilism, in all its reasonings, abides in a region of mist and darkness; but Theology is the parent region of light, and truth, and love.

Three alternative views have been held concerning the nature of matter; that it is continuous, solid, extended, and infinitely divisible; that it consists of solid, discrete, but extended atoms, endued with various forces, and with a large amount of porous interstice or interval between them; and that it consists of centres of attractive and repulsive forces alone. The first is the popular view, before close attention to the facts of science, the second is that of Newton, the third of Boscovich. All of these alike, in "First Principles," are declared to be unthinkable and inconceivable, though the resulting nescience is strangely and silently transferred from Physics to Theology. But in truth all of them are thinkable, or we could not contrast them, analyze their consequences, and compare them together. The contrast, I believe, is this. The two former result from the absence of close analysis, or from imperfect analysis, of the phenomena, and involve some internal inconsistency and contradiction. The third results from the whole drift and scope of modern scientific progress. It implies a fundamental mystery, but no contradiction. On the contrary, it supplies a definite basis for clear and exact reasoning, and is alone really consistent, definite, and intelligible.

The view is owned to be ingenious, and to elude various difficulties, but two or three objections are urged as decisive. First, that it points to what we cannot represent in thought, and sets out with what is inconceivable. "A centre of force without extension is unthinkable; we can form nothing more than a symbolic conception of the illegitimate order."

The truth, I conceive, is just the reverse. An extended centre of forces, that vary by any law of distance, is what is really unthinkable; since they would then have to vary by a law of distance, with no definite distance by which they can be defined. On the other hand, the present conception is one with which all mathematicians are familiar. It lies at the very basis of those theories of Newton, to which, and not at all to Atheistic Positivism, Astronomy chiefly owes its immense progress in the last two hundred years. It is definite in itself, and also in the results which flow from it, when particular laws of force are assumed. It is thus a symbolic conception of the most legitimate kind, and indeed it will be hard to prove that any other is equally legitimate. The strict continuity of matter is disproved by all the facts of modern chemical science. The middle hypothesis of extended, solid atoms, not in contact, separated by mere space, and kept apart by repulsive forces, combines all the metaphysical difficulty of centres of force with the real contradiction of the opposite extreme. For these atoms must by the hypothesis be continuous, infinitely divisible in conception, and yet, from some unexplained cause, not actually divisible. On the other hand, since they do not touch, but are kept asunder by forces which emanate from them, while they are treated as indivisible wholes, we have the mental contradiction of forces varying by no law of distance, because the distances are infinitely manifold at the same moment, and of a solid structure never called into exercise at all, and on which the phenomena cannot therefore really depend.

Two further objections are offered to this third view of the constitution of matter. First, that the idea of resistance cannot be separated from that of an extended body which resists. But here words are mistaken for things, a compound for a simple idea, and a simple for a compound. When physics were less advanced, matter was usually defined by solidity and extension, and on this was founded the corpuscular philosophy. A compound and highly complex property of aggregations of matter, in the mutable form most familiar to our senses, was mistaken for its true definition. There was thus a threefold error of excess and defect. Matter was confounded with pore or intervening space. Solidity, a mutable result of aggregation under certain conditions, was mistaken for defining essence. Force, also, one essential element in a true definition, was omitted wholly. The advance of chemical science, of optics and electricity, has cut the ground from under the feet of this spurious definition. But still the view cleaves in part, as a superstition of science, even to those with whom the belief in a God is a superstition of theology. This seems the true source of error in the above statement. Solid resistance is not a simple property, but highly compound; since exact science proves that seeming is not real contact, and takes place at distances capable of an imperfect estimation. It consists in the sudden action of strong repulsion, which will not yield to manual pressure, when the hand, or some other solid held by it, approaches very near to some given extended surface. A crystal of salt thus resists. But increase the pressure to a certain limit, and it yields, and crumbles beneath it. Melt the crystal in water, and the matter remains, but all its power of solid resistance has disappeared. Again, the idea of a repellent force, emanating from a point only, and not from a sensible, solid, and extended surface, is familiar and easy. It is seen constantly in the mutual action of a pair of magnetic needles. And the fact that seeming is not real contact, but depends on the action of intense repulsive forces at minute distances, is one of the most certain in the whole range of Modern Physics.

But the chemical law of Definite Proportions, it is urged, is impossible except on the condition of ultimate atoms, and thus Newton's theory is at least preferable to that of Boscovich. A strange inversion of the real truth. The theory of extended solid atoms is reconcilable, no doubt, with this great chemical fact. But it serves chiefly to disguise its real simplicity, and to load it with unscientific, arbitrary, and variable elements. The atomic weight of each chemical element will then depend on four or five causes all arbitrary, the figure, length, breadth, depth, and specific density of its solid atom, to which number will be added in compound atoms. On the other hand, the theory of force-centres explains the same fact in the simplest possible way, without any arbitrary element. The combining weight in any chemical atom, simple or compound, will be fixed by the number of its force-centres, or monads, alone.

The simple chemical atom will be the first step of composition beyond the monad, and thus the most permanent, and least subject to dissolution; while compound chemical atoms will form later stages of a like reunion.

Two further mistakes of no slight importance on the same subject need to be removed. First, it is said that the law of the inverse square, in gravitation, light, and electricity, is a necessary result of the conditions of space. And next, that central forces, conforming necessarily to this law, can produce only a state of indifference or equilibrium. The first remark is a fundamental error. It is true that impulses or actions, gradually propagated through a medium, as in luminous or electric waves, tend, by the conditions of space, to diminish as the inverse square. But this result is approximate, not exact, and could only obtain perfectly, if the medium were both continuous and homogeneous. It is also liable to vary, and in these cases probably does vary, with the angular direction; and being also successive in time, must vary with every change of the original impulse. Thus the law of the inverse square enters only as one factor, modified by several others. But gravitation, so far as science has detected, is instantaneous, and not transmitted in time, even with the speed of light; for this would introduce modifications which experience disproves. And it is so clearly not due to necessity, that its discovery arose from a careful comparison of the effects of several other laws of force, equally possible in themselves; and from a proof, by strict reasoning, that of these many conceivable laws that of the inverse square alone agrees with the orbit of the moon round the earth, with Kepler's two laws, and other facts of celestial observation. And this disproves the second argument against the theory of force-centres. It is true that the law of the inverse square alone can never account for material structure and solidity. But the phenomena of light, and of chemical attraction prove clearly that other laws must exist, one of mutual repulsion, by which the elasticity of the medium of light is sustained, and another of cohesive attraction, increasing more rapidly than as the inverse square, and on which the permanence of chemical structure, and mechanical solidity, as well as crystalline figure, must depend.

This view of the constitution of matter, to which all the progress of modern discovery rapidly tends, far from being unthinkable, has already been thought out and reasoned upon in various works, and is capable of being further unfolded, in a definite and scientific manner, with every variety in the laws of central force assumed to exist. And this same conception, the ripest growth of modern science, both on its side of experiment and mathematical deduction, seems to throw some light on the kindred subject, the nature of material creation.

Two views of creation have often struggled for mastery, the formation of matter out of nothing, and its evolution from the self-existent Being. Divines have usually inclined to the former view, philosophers to the second. The former is open to the grave difficulty, how can a mere negation ever become something? The latter, again, seems to destroy the contrast between God and the universe, making the latter a part of God himself.

Now the view of matter here maintained, which has strong evidence in its favour from modern science alone, combines the half-truths in these opposite views of creation, and harmonizes them together. A point, without force, is a mere negation of being and even of extension; but is distinguished by position from all other points, and may be defined "an individuated possibility of being." Force, a power of attraction upon all other centres, is the direct gift of the Creator, the Fountain of power in all its forms from the highest to the lowest. Thus the nothing becomes a something, a definite something, with definite powers of action towards every other monad, simultaneously called into being by the creative fiat of the Almighty. Its active power is the direct gift of God, but its individuality depends on its position, as one amongst the threefold infinitude of possibilities of being, which are summed up in the vague expression, Infinite Space. The possible laws of central force are various, and even the actual laws, it seems highly probable, are not single, but dual, plural, or manifold. And hence the selection of these laws, resulting from no necessity, implies and requires the choice and will of the First Cause, the Intelligent and All-Wise Creator. But these laws, once assigned, will define the gift of being in its lowest form. These atoms, by their active force, resemble the Creator by whom it is bestowed, and from whom their being arose; but in all other respects they are a contrast. They are multitudinous, almost to infinity of number, and He is One. They are, in the centre which individuates them, a point, a negation of all being, a bare capability of being raised into being by a gift of power inseparably linked with that original nothing. They represent the extreme of littleness and emptiness, while the Creator is the opposite extreme of absolute and eternal fulness. They are mutable, acted upon and moved to and fro by the force of every other atom, while He is free from all passiveness, the Supreme and Perfect Activity. The ripest discoveries, and latest tendencies of science only tend to place in a clearer light the perfections of the great I AM, the Fountain of all power, who spake and it was done, and of whom it is written—" Of Him, and through Him, and to Him, are all things, to whom be glory for ever. Amen!"

## CHAPTER VI.

### ON INFINITE SPACE.

The doctrine that Matter is created, the result of a work of divine will and power, has been obscured or denied by reasonings drawn from our conceptions of Space. The creation of Matter, it has sometimes been urged, requires us to hold the creation of Space also, which is said to be inconceivable.

In "First Principles," where this argument occurs, it agrees ill with the chapter on Ultimate Scientific Ideas, which presently follows. All the alternatives, that Space is subjective, and a form of thought only; that it is a nonentity, an attribute, a real entity, and thus either finite or infinite, are affirmed in turn to be unthinkable and inconceivable. How, then, can we safely infer, in such darkness, that it is an external entity, needing creation as much as Matter, or that its creation is harder to conceive than its bare existence alone? Still the conception of Space as a real existence, prior to Matter, and independent of the Divine will, seems often to be a covert defence of Atheistic Materialism. If this mighty void, Infinite Space, has a real and necessary existence before any creation, and wholly independent of the Creator, is it much harder to conceive that Matter, the shifting and variable contents of this Infinite Space, may also be uncreated, and exist from all eternity?

Here three main questions arise. Is Space only subjective, a form of thought, or objective, that is, either an entity, or some relation or attribute of things themselves? If objective, has it a separable existence, or is it an inseparable relation or attribute of material objects alone? Have we any distinct conception of Infinite Space, and this as necessary, so that to conceive its non-existence is impossible?

The doctrine of Kant, that Space is a subjective form of thought, is adopted by Sir W. Hamilton in these words —" Space is a necessary condition of thought, and may be considered in itself, and in the things it contains. It is positively inconceivable as a whole, either infinitely unbounded, or positively bounded, either infinitely divisible, or absolutely indivisible. It is positively conceivable as a mean between these extremes, either as an indefinite whole, or an indefinite part, for thus

K

it is relative. Space applies proximately to things considered as Substance. Extension, being a condition of positive thinking, clings to all our conceptions, and it is one merit of the Philosophy of the Conditioned, that it proves space to be only a law of thought, not a law of things. Our inability to conceive an absolute elimination from space of aught we have conceived to occupy space, gives the law of what I have called Ultimate Incompressibility" (Discourse, pp. 142, 143).

The strictures on this theory in Mr. Spencer's Psychology seem to be clear, forcible, and decisive.

"It is curious to see a doctrine, which positively contradicts our primary conceptions, chosen as a refuge from another, which simply doubts them. In the philosophy of Kant, however, this is done. Scepticism merely questions all things, and professes to affirm nothing. Kant, in anxiety to escape from it, decisively affirms things contrary to universal belief. That Space and Time are 'subjective conditions of thought,' which have no objective basis, is as repugnant to common sense as any proposition that can be formed. To adopt it instead of the one, that we have no sufficient evidence of any external existence, seems a preference of the greater evil to the less. The fact on which Kant bases his assertion that Space is a subjective form, not an objective reality, namely, that we can conceive the annihilation of bodies, not of space, is quite comprehensible on the hypothesis that all knowledge is from without ... We know Space has an ability to contain bodies. If so, the fact that we cannot conceive its annihilation is quite accountable on the experience hypothesis. We can conceive bodies annihilated, because by evaporation or burning we have seen them annihilated, that is, to our senses. But the ability to contain bodies we cannot conceive annihilated, because we have never known it absent. . Granting his whole position, Kant has no higher guarantee for his inference than the Universal Postulate. The thing *must* be, he says; and the meaning of this *must* is, that no other thing can be conceived. Having assumed the validity of this canon, what does he do? He forthwith asserts what the canon denies, and denies what it asserts. The subjectivity of Time and Space being irresistible, he says, as an inference, he asserts it as a fact. But to receive it as a fact involves two impossibilities, the forming concepts of Time and Space as subjective forms, and the abolition of the concepts as objective icalities Kant's proposition is both unthinkable in itself, and immediately involves an unthinkable consequence. Think of Space, the thing, and think of Self, that which is conscious. Having clearly realized them, put the two together, and conceive the one as the property of the other. What results? Nothing but a conflict of two thoughts that cannot be united. It would be as practicable to imagine a round square."

It is easier, in fact, to fly by an effort of will, than by a like effort to conceive the space we should have to fly through, as a form of thought in our own mind, and not something external. The one is merely a physical inability, which the structure of a bird would enable us to overcome. The other is a mental contradiction, which, in whatever way we try to realize it, remains inconceivable.

Common sense and true philosophy are thus agreed in the fact that Space is something perceived and known without us, and no subjective "form of thought" to the mind itself, in contrast to the doctrine of Kant and all his followers. Our conviction of this fact is just as clear as of any single step in the argument which would disprove it, and even clearer than most of them. But if objective, is it an entity, an attribute, or a relation? In his "First Principles," Mr. Spencer deserts and nullifies his own reasoning in his Psychology, and affirms every alternative alike to be unthinkable, so that by his own principle it should be rejected as untrue. The true answer is not far to seek, and very simple. We do not conceive of mere space as an actual being, like objects contained in it, nor as an attribute or inherent power or quality of those objects, but as a definite relation between them, or the parts of them. This relation has definite characters, which the mind can no more reverse than it can disbelieve the objective realities themselves, and is conceived to be independent of those details of place, character, and form, whereby the material objects are differenced from each other. Space, then, is the summation of all those relations of distance, forward or backward, sideways, up or down, in which bodies are either known to be placed, or conceived to be placeable, one towards another.

A third inquiry bears more directly on the Theistic argument. Have we so fixed and positive a conception of Infinite Space, as to make its non-existence inconceivable? Is it an independent something, prior to creation, existing by necessity, and throughout a successive past eternity? Such an opinion, if received as a certain truth, may well prepare the mind to admit, as conceivable, and almost as probable, the uncreated self-existence of matter also

Now, first, it is plainly impossible to form any visual or sensible conception of Infinite Space. For the same is true of a space far less than infinite. When we gaze on the sky, the sensible impression is only of a distance, at the most, of a few miles, which is clear from the fact that, with an horizon of ten or fifteen miles, the hemisphere is seen as a flattened arch. Our knowledge of the stars, as immensely more remote, requires a separate effort of thought, and does not combine with the sensible view of the firmament into one consistent whole. The imagination, then, has no conception at all of Infinite Space. It is an inference, true or false, of the understanding alone.

Secondly, our reason itself can form no conception of space at all, as wholly independent of matter, and the position of material objects. We know it, and learn of it first of all, by the relations of place among terrestrial objects. Next, we see that this relation remains unchanged, so long as the limiting and outmost objects exist, however many the changes, however few the objects within the limits, or even if they disappear entirely, and are replaced by imaginary lines. But when we strive to contemplate space, wholly apart from matter, or any material way-mark or boundary, the effort is vain. The usual limit of our attempts is one of two alternatives. Either we picture to ourselves a spherical surface, placing ourselves in the centre, and conceive this boundary to recede farther and farther, or else we borrow from geometry of three dimensions, and conceive of three lines, crossing each other at right angles, and stretching onward without limit on every side. But to conceive of Infinite Space, or even of space extending indefinitely, without actual matter, or some imaginary substitute, so far material as to be sensible to the eye, will be found, I think, wholly impossible.

Infinite Space, if this be true, is so far from being, in a strict sense, conceived as necessary, independent, eternal, that it is removed from this character by a double and triple contrast. We have no conviction, natural or acquired, of the necessary existence of matter, but the reverse. We have no power to conceive of space at all, wholly apart from matter, that is, apart from real material objects, or else from some surface or lines, conceived to exist at the same time, whether a firmament or geometrical co-ordinates. And these are conceived also to have the material property of acting like a coloured surface, or threads of light, upon the organs of vision. We have no power of picturing space as positively infinite, or even of so conceiving it by the help of reason, but only the negative infinity of adding to the finite more and more. On the other hand, we cannot conceive of material objects at all, except as in relations of place to each other and to ourselves. Thus, Finite Space, a brief expression for the sum of all these relations, is conceived as co-existing necessarily with the whole material world. Next, we conceive of these relations as unaltered by the presence, absence, or varied motions of the bodies contained in this space, so long as the outmost limits are unchanged. Thirdly, beyond the outer limits known by experience, or guessed at by inference, or conceived, for the moment, by the imagination as now existing, we are compelled to feel that other like objects might exist; and also that relations of place, involving a possible enlargement of finite space, would inevitably and inseparably attend such an existence. And thus we arrive at a clear and definite conclusion, by which the mist of ambiguous and misleading phrases may in part be cleared away. Finite Space consists in a mental integration, free from other elements, of all the place-relations between the world, matter, and atoms of an actual material universe. Infinite Space adds to this no positive reality whatever. It simply condenses into one phrase the double conviction, from which we cannot escape, that, however vast the actual universe, it is finite, and its enlargement in its own nature possible, and next, that place-relations are inseparable from this possible, as well as from the actual, creation. It means, in brief, that extension in space is an essential relation of all created matter; and that the same relation must accompany the material creation through every conceivable stage of possible increase, to which our minds are unable to assign any absolute limit.

Our conceptions of space, when closely examined, will be found to confirm and strengthen the Theistic argument in four different ways.

First, space has three dimensions, and neither less nor more. We cannot, by any effort of mind, conceive a universe of two dimensions, or one only. This threefold character, of length, breadth, and height or depth, insoparably combined in one, is the main character of the space-conception, and gives rise to that well-known branch of abstract science, the geometry of three dimensions. This hypothetical necessity cleaves to matter, in all the possible variety of forms and characters it may assume, and gives birth to a vast and large variety of geometrical and certain truths. And thus, in those relations of lifeless matter, which are the most abstract, definite, and unalterable, there is a triunity which forms the basis of the whole. The highest mystery of Revealed Theology has a direct counterpart at the very basement of the whole universe of created being. This mighty illimitable ocean of space, the grand receptacle for the shifting, countless phenomena of the material universe, has thus a blue sky of eternal truth bending over it, whose image it reflects clearly evermore in its tranquil bosom.

Next, place is essentially relative and dependent. Let us conceive a single spherical ball alone in creation, without any other object around, above, beside, or below. In such a case we shall find even its motion inconceivable. Deal with it as we please, it is just as it was before, one sole object in the midst of an infinitude of possible places, extending on every side. Where nothing is changed there is no motion, and the possibility of motion ceases, when there is nothing to or from which a thing can be moved. Extend the conception to the whole finite universe, and the result is the same. It cannot be moved, as a whole, because there is nothing to which the motion can be referred. But suppose a new universe created, outside the first, and motion is possible in either, being now referred to the other. Motion and place are thus essentially relative. But this relativity suggests inevitably the correlative conception of some Absolute Being, not localized in a particular place, on which, or on whom, it depends. However vast, we cannot conceive of the universe as actually more than finite; and this finite, however vast, compels our thoughts to look higher for the cause of its being, and of the limitations of its being, to One who is Infinite.

In the third place, however vast the actual universe, we can conceive of its possible increase. It is impossible for us to stay at any point, and say to ourselves,—So far actual material being extends, but there our thoughts find a fixed barrier, and we cannot conceive that it should ever pass this limit, and range further. To the actual universe, however immense its real dimensions may be, we are compelled to add the thought of a possible universe, which might or may hereafter come into being, with no limit assignable to this later increase. But this idea of the possible, lying beyond the actual, awakens irresistibly the conception of necessary being on the other side. The actual, that might not have been, suggests itself to the mind as midway between the necessary, which must be, and cannot but be, and the possible, which may never come into being. It is not the actual universe alone, by its limitation and relativity in place, but the vast possible extensions of that universe, the void place beyond, which is nothing but a possibility of relations of distance between atoms or worlds not now created, which suggest the idea of a Divine Power, an uncreated Author and Lord of the universe, as their only possible solution.

But, lastly, the idea of space forces on us the conception of a Divine Being, the great I AM, by compelling us, the more calmly we reflect, to recognize more plainly a true and proper Infinite. Let us conceive an abscissa or ordinate stretching on without limits right and left, from a given point. Let us conceive two points on each side, first coinciding at a unit of distance from the centre, but moving outward and inward, so that one distance is always the reciprocal of the other; or so that a distance three, four, five times greater corresponds to one three, four, five times less. The two outer points diverge more and more, the others approach at opposite sides to the centre between them. So long as the greater distance is finite, however large, the other is finite, however small, and the direction right and left of the centre remains common to both on each side. But let the smaller distance vanish, the points coinciding with the centre, and the outer distance becomes infinite, and the distinction of right and left disappears at the same moment. The positive and the negative infinite are the same. The same is true in length, forward and backward, and in height, up or down. When the minor points coincide in the centre the six directions right and left, before and behind, up and down, all coincide, and the answering infinite must coincide also. The manner of this is inconceivable, it is true; but the fact is demonstrable. The true Infinite with reference to space is neither here nor there, is equally related to all dimensions alike, answers to the mathematical point in unity, simplicity, and impartiality of reference to all directions and distances, and differs from it by this one contrast, that one is all-exclusive, the other all-inclusive. But such an absolute fulness, with reference to place, unlike the point which is manifold, and capable of infinitude of number, requires an Absolute Being, whose relation to the universe is expressed thereby. Infinite Space, in the negative sense, denotes only the possibility of extension in a finite, material universe. But in its positive sense, in which the Absolute and the Infinite coincide and are reconciled, it is and can be nothing else than the Omnipresence of the One True and Infinite God, in reference to the whole range of that mighty universe, which His wisdom guides, and His power has called into being.

# CHAPTER VII

### ON FORCE, LAW, AND NECESSITY.

THE main contrast between the Christian doctrine of Creation and the theories of modern scepticism turns on the three subjects of Law, Force, and Necessity. Is Force a metaphysical idea to be cast aside, that we may deal with phenomena and their laws, apart from useless abstractions, pure and alone? Must we admit forces, as well as laws of force, but as uncreated, necessary, and eternal? Or do forces and laws of force depend on the First Cause, the Fountain of all power, the Supreme Lawgiver? Do they contain clear signs, in their own nature, of contingent, originated, and dependent existence? The leading sceptics are not agreed, and offer contradictory substitutes for the ancient creed of Scripture and the whole Church, that "in the beginning God created the heavens and the earth."

The power and wisdom of the Creator reveal themselves more brightly, the higher we mount in the scale of created being. Man is higher than animals, animals than plants, and plants than lifeless matter. But, on the other hand, the question is simpler and less embarrassed, before we rise to the mystery of life, in that lower field which refers to matter and the medium of light alone. The complexity of nature increases as we rise, and the precise nature of living force remains still very obscure. The unknown bears here a still greater proportion to the known, and thus leaves a wider range for unbelieving theories, which can hide themselves amidst the countless facts and guesses of physiology, like Adam in Paradise, from the unwelcome presence of the living God. It is well, then, to view this question of law and force in connexion with the simpler sciences of astronomy, optics, and chemistry, before passing on to the higher field.

The doctrine of the Positive Philosophy was thus stated by its author, forty-six years ago, in a paper republished by him in the fourth volume of his system of Political Science.

"Man has begun by conceiving phenomena of all kinds as due to the direct and constant influence of supernatural agents. Next, he has considered them as produced by different abstract Forces, inherent in bodies, but distinct and heterogeneous. Lastly, he has confined himself to viewing them as subject to a certain number of invincible natural Laws, which are nothing else but the general expression of the relations observed in their development. All those who know sufficiently the state of the human mind at different epochs of civilization, will easily verify the correctness of this general fact. A very simple observation will confirm it. The education of the individual, so far as spontaneous, presents necessarily the same phases as those of the race. Now every man, who is up to the level of his age, will easily recognize in himself that he has been, naturally, a theologian in infancy, a metaphysician in his youth, and a physicist in his manhood. The history of the sciences proves that it has been the same with the race at large" (Système de Pol. Pos. vol. iv. App. p. 137).

The age, to whose level an appeal is here made as the universal standard, seems, in the view of M. Comte, to consist of those exclusively, who have cast off all religious faith with their nursery clothes. This experience, however, is not universal, even in France in the nineteenth century, and far less in other lands. The Positive Philosophy, in fact, is the Inductive Philosophy of Lord Bacon, baptized anew, with no Christian baptism, in the troubled

L

waters of the French Revolution, enriched with a skilful, though imperfect, classification of sciences, but claiming for its especial merit a new theory of scientific progress. Its inductive character is borrowed from Lord Bacon, and shared fully by Descartes, Boyle, Pascal, Newton, and other great Christian philosophers of the last three centuries. Its extrusion of Theology, as unknowable, from the list of sciences, it shares with other kindred schools of scepticism, and even with the Philosophy of the Unconditioned. Its arrangement of the sciences is good, though imperfect, when Theology is once restored to its true place; though one still better has been provided long ago, in the first page of Scripture, for thoughtful and reverent minds. But its theory of progress, as stated above, from Theology, through Metaphysics, to Positivism and Religious Nihilism, is its chief engine of assault on the doctrine of Creation, and on all theological truth. It involves two main questions, the relation of religious faith and metaphysical ideas to the inductions of science.

This theory, in its reference to the so-called theological stage, involves three main errors. Theism, Polytheism, and Fetichism, are strangely grouped together under the name

of Theology, as three hypotheses invented to
account for the facts of daily experience, and
to increase men's knowledge of the outward
world, and their power over its changes. This
is a wholly false view of their nature. Man
has a twofold instinct, of dominion over nature, which he was formed to rule, and of
fear and reverence toward the Unseen and Unknown. One instinct prompts the researches of
natural science, the other all acts of religious
faith and worship. The first, divorced from
the second, issues in unbelieving pride; the
second, without the first, in slavish and blind
superstition. When combined in healthy union,
they lead to manly and intelligent dominion
over nature, and reverent and holy worship of
God. Fetichism and Polytheism result from
the up-looking of the soul, when diseased or
feeble; so that it stops short in the worship of
secondary powers, below the First Cause, the
Supreme, or even turns aside to worship powers
of evil. Theism results from the same up-looking of the soul, when healthy and perfect, so
as never to rest till it gazes on the Only Wise,
the Supremely Good. Positivism is the result
of human pride, when it refuses to look upward
at all, and fixes its thoughts only on man himself, or what is placed beneath him, the brute

L. 2

creation and lifeless matter. It is an extreme of this blindness, when the True and Eternal God, the false gods of classic heathenism, and the fetiches of savage tribes, are grouped in one class, and viewed alike as mere tools invented by men, in different stages of progress, to assist them in gaining mastery over the future changes of the outer world.

It is a second error, that Theism, Polytheism, and Fetichism are grouped together, in contrast to Metaphysics and Positivism, as forming one theological stage. The contrast between Judaism and old heathenism, between Christianity and the paganism of the first centuries, is far greater than between these last and modern Positivism, which very rapidly grew, in the hands of its founder, into a revival of old heathenism in a modern form. The intense conflict between Jewish worship of Jehovah and heathen idolatry is the main fact of Old Testament history. The like contrast was no less marked in the three centuries of heathen persecution of the Gospel. Obscured for a time during the decline of the Church into a semblance of paganism, it broke out anew at the era of the Reformation. Positivism, on the other hand, had not finished its destructive work, as opposed to all Christian faith, when it blossomed, in the hands of its founder, into a new religion of humanity. And the affinities of this new creed are very plain. Rejecting the pure Monotheism of Protestant countries with deep aversion, it claims to revive and perfect early Fetichism and Polytheism, and also to recast into a modern shape the saint and virgin worship of Roman Catholic lands.

The classification, then, in this law of progress has a double fault. It strives to blot out and obscure a deep and fundamental contrast, proved by long ages of strife, between the Theology of the Old and New Testament and the countless mythologies of heathenism, and it erects into a ripened stage of human progress a new heathenish creed of its own. Its Neorotheism differs from the old Polytheism only as the cold-blooded from the warm-blooded animals, being really an artificial revival of the worship of dead men and dead women on the largest scale.

It is a third error, though one less important, to assume that Christian faith in the God of the Bible has no direct bearing on the later progress of natural science. Such, indeed, is not its main object. No sincere and devout Christian can believe in God and Christ, merely as a graving tool to help him in perfecting the natural sciences. But still their progress has certainly been aided by faith in a Supreme Designer, the Lord of the whole universe. Final causes, even in Physics, and still more in Physiology, have not been wholly sterile. No heathen or infidel, but a devout Christian, discovered the law of universal gravitation. That grand, simple law was more likely to be attained by a believer in One God of universal dominion, than by a believer in gods many, with separate dominions in heaven, earth, and sea; or by one who turns millions of transformed insects on our planet into the factors of his complex "Supreme Being," the objects of a strange and novel worship. The discovery of the circulation of the blood, by Harvey, one main advance in Physiology, was directly owing to his recognition of final causes; and the same is true, to a great extent, of those researches of Cuvier, which opened a new stage of geological progress. Even on the side of human and natural science, true religious faith "hath the promise of the life that now is, as well as of that which is to come."

But a wider question remains. Can science advance by observing phenomena alone, without including ideas of law, force, and causation? Can it separate the idea of law from those of force and causation, counting the first inductive, the second metaphysical and obscure? Or can it deal both with law and force, and still exclude causes as metaphysical, and claim, on the strength of this contrast, to open a new and perfect stage of true philosophy?

"The Positive Philosophy, dismissing every search for the *cause*, which it proclaims inaccessible to the human mind, aims exclusively to discover the *law*, that is, the constant relations of likeness and succession which the facts have among themselves" (App p 144) Such is the definition of his theory, proposed early by its own founder Is he able, then, consistently, to confine himself to the notion of law, and to dispense with all mention of causes, forces, and powers? The context is a full reply. In the third part of the same Appendix, which comes just before these definitions, within ninety pages those forbidden ideas recur almost two hundred times So deeply seated are they in the instincts of the human mind, so inwrought into the whole texture of language, that every effort to uproot them only proves their irrepressible vitality

Again, is the notion of law, as binding phenomena together, less mysterious than that of force and causation, which it is designed to exclude? How are these laws to be defined? Are they nothing more than a mere apposition of phenomena by thousands, without referring them to any material objects, to which they belong? How then can they need discovering, or explain any thing when discovered? Are they like the outer bands, which bind together many ears of corn in one sheaf, or like some common stem, of which the separate phenomena are branches? Are they entities or nonentities? Subjective modes of thought, in viewing the facts, or objective realities in the facts themselves? In answering these questions, the disciples of Positivism are sorely perplexed, and their oscillations are extreme. The author of the "History of Civilization," within a few pages, in the text and the foot-notes, propounds views diametrically opposed. In one place he reminds his readers that these laws are purely mental conceptions, convenient groupings of the phenomena, and have no reality or meaning beyond the facts themselves. In the other, soon after, from the recorded number of London suicides for five or six years, he infers a law of self-destruction so omnipotent, that no amount of education, and no spread of religious faith, can hinder a fixed percentage of mankind from putting themselves to death. These laws of nature are thus, by turns, verbal nonentities, and a friendly brotherhood of omnipotent deities.

The idea of force, according to M Comte, is wholly foreign to the Positive Philosophy, and belongs entirely to the bygone metaphysical stage. But Dr. Tyndall, one of the most celebrated physical experimenters of the same non-Christian school, in his censure of the clergy, as noble savages in their supposed ignorance of science, exactly reverses the definition M. Comte has given "The scientific mind," he says, "can find no rest in the mere registration of sequence in nature. The further question intrudes with resistless might—whence comes the sequence? What is it that binds the consequent with its antecedent in nature? The truly scientific intellect never can obtain rest until it reaches the *forces*, by which the observed succession is produced It was thus with Torricelli, it was thus with Newton it is thus pre-eminently with the real scientific men of to-day." (Tyndall, *Fortn. R*, June, 1867, p. 657) The statement is true. But the arrow aimed at a venture, and drawn at full strength to smite down the clergy for their ignorance of science, really smites to the heart that Positive Philosophy to which the writer seems in other respects to belong. The deep instinct which passes from phenomena to forces by which they are caused, and which Positivism claims for one of its chief merits to set aside and destroy, is here declared to be the foundation of all true philosophy.

The idea of law, in physics, is plainly borrowed from the higher field of politics and social science. In its proper sense it implies a lawgiver, sovereign, or legislature, by whom acts are prohibited, or a course of action enjoined; a class or series of acts commanded or forbidden; sanctions or penalties for disobedience; and subjects, with power of action and choice, by whom the law is obeyed or broken. In physics it is clear that all these elements of the parent idea cannot be retained. Hence there must be risk of great ambiguity. A law, with no law-giver to impose it, no sanction for its observance, no power of choice in its subjects, no consciousness that it is observed, no possibility of being transgressed, becomes the most subtle and evanescent of metaphysical abstractions, if not the most misleading and delusive of terms. There seem to be four varieties of the sceptical hypothesis, which need separate examination. To fix our ideas, the first law of Kepler, deduced from observations of the planet Mars and the discovery of his elliptic orbit, may be a convenient illustration.

First, on M. Comte's exposition of his great maxim, law must exclude every conception of cause and force, and means only "the constant relations of similitude and succession, which the facts have among themselves." The essential conception of law, as involving control of some kind or other, is here set aside and entirely perishes. But the misnomer, except for the risk of confusion, matters little, if only a true principle is given under a false name. The facts, on this view, are the phenomena, the successive visual appearances of Mars on the same night, or on successive nights; for substance is a metaphysical conception, which the Positive Philosophy positively forbids and excludes. The relation of succession is seen in the visual impressions on the eye of the observer in the same night, that of similitude in their resemblance one to another. Hence the first step of progress is to believe them effects of one and the same cause, a luminous object, the planet Mars. But this first step implies a cause, a force, and a being, acting from afar on the organ of sight; remaining the same, while the visual impressions are repeated every moment. These are metaphysical ideas which Positivism would exclude. Next the visual impressions of one night succeed those of another night, and resemble them. Yet the resemblance is imperfect. One night may be clear and another cloudy. The place among the stars will be rather different, the position at the same hour will differ widely. How can the next step be taken by numbering phenomena, and noting their sequence alone? Positivism, having proscribed metaphysics, is smitten with palsy, and cannot move. You have the relations of sequence, resemblance, and partial unlikeness, but no means for reasoning from them. Once again we must call in the aid of a metaphysical idea, permanent substance, and of two geometrical ideas that belong to substances, not to phenomena that expire as soon as born, namely place and motion. The phenomena of one night suggest a common subject to which they belong, and by which they are caused. This object, whether disc or globe may be still unknown, can be conceived as moving in space. As a substance, not a heap of phenomena, we can compare its positions, and we discover one motion common to the stars, which accounts for the nightly difference of position at the same hour, and a slighter change with reference to the stars around. Thus we name it a star from the observations of similitude in a single night; and we distinguish it as a planet, a moving star, from its detected change of place on different nights. But we have still no conception of its distance. By degrees we find that it is more distant than the clouds, more distant than the moon behind which it disappears. At every stage of advancing science we have to treat it as a real body, a globe, not a disc, since its face varies, and it is always round; a globe lighted by the sun, not self-luminous, since the telescope shows that it is not always full, but sometimes gibbous only; a globe revolving in an orbit most excentric with regard to the earth, as proved by the variations of the disc in size, but when the data are treated by geometry, much less excentric, and almost circular, when referred to the sun. Every step in this advance requires us to leave the phenomena, as separate, momentary impressions on the visual sense; and to deal with the planet as a globe of matter, moving in space, having a countless number of definite relations, never actually observed, with the sun, the moon, the other planets, and other parts of the earth, where no observations have been made. We must exchange mere phenomena for substance—material substance of definite shape, form, and place, acted on by the light of the sun, and acting in turn by the light it receives on the eye of every observer, child, peasant, or astronomer, before we can take a single step upward in the ascent of science.

Again, was the law of Kepler discovered by tracing relations of similitude and succession among the phenomena, that is, the visual impressions, night after night, and moment after moment, on the retina of each separate observer? On the contrary, the phenomena had to be put out of sight, and the planet itself to be contemplated in a new set of relations, witnessed by no human eye; as a globe, moving in empty space around the sun, a still mightier globe, in one level plane, of which the distances, the angles, and the times, alone were considered. This transfer of thought from the phenomena to an ideal picture was needful, before the great discovery could be made. No geometry could have solved the problem, or divined the secret, if directly applied to the series of phenomena alone. For these vary by an infinity of moments of observation, by ten thousand observers and their points of sight, the double motions of the earth and of the planet, the state of the atmosphere, and shifting clouds of the sky. The phenomenal complexity is well nigh infinite. The law was reached by five main steps of upward ascent; and science mounted higher and higher at each step, by dealing with abiding substance, not with momentary, shadowy phenomena alone.

Physical Laws, then, far from excluding ideas of substance, force, and cause, as affirmed by Positivism, include them, and depend upon them, in every stage of scientific progress. They are its secret vital power. Withdraw them, and science is smitten with palsy, and cannot move. The deep instinct, which looks beyond phenomena to forces on which they depend, is truly said by Dr. Tyndall to be the mainspring of all true science in modern as in ancient times. But there are still three ways in which a Divine Lawgiver and Creator may be excluded, when the ideas of force, and laws of force, are both received. The series of changes may be personified and deified, so as to make them a law to themselves. Matter may be spiritualized, and made to impose a motion on itself, and guide its own movements by a conscious plan. Or lastly, nature, the whole universe, may be deified, or turned into a Supreme

Fate, which compels every part to obey the decrees of the mighty whole.

The first view seems to come nearest to M. Comte's own definition, and merely supplies, in the phenomena themselves, and their sequence, that missing element of power or control, which is the essence of law, and without which it must disappear entirely. This variety seems to have been held, at least for the moment, by the author of the "History of Civilization," when he ascribed to averages of suicide for a few years such immense power to establish a settled percentage of self-destruction, that no restraints of social law or religious feeling could ever overcome them. Yet of all varieties it seems the most unmeaning and unreasonable. A series of events has no existence, till the last of them has occurred. It is just as easy to conceive a man the parent of his own grandfather, as to make a series of phenomena the lawgiver over the events of which it is composed. Can the ellipse described by the planet Mars be itself the law which prescribes and causes the actual revolution? But the ellipse is nothing, before it is described, but a possible pathway; an empty space, a series of relations of place between positions which may be occupied in succession, and no actual reality.

To deify matter is a vast absurdity, to deify empty space a deeper folly still; but the apotheosis of a mathematical line would seem to be nearly the climax of all possible unreason. "A definite combination" in like manner, "of heterogeneous changes, simultaneous and successive, in correspondence with external co-existences and sequences" may be honoured with the name of Life. But on this view nothing can be alive at all, till it has lived on for some indefinite period; which is just the same in a higher science, as to make the ellipse of Mars the cause and parent of the motion by which the planet fulfils its elliptic revolution. The strides of a race-horse a year hence are thus included in the definition of the vital force, by which he lives to-day.

The control, then, which satisfies the conception of law, since it cannot reside in the whole series of the phenomena, may be referred to the matter itself, as determining its own movements. This plainly, under the name of philosophy, would revive the fetichism of savage tribes and of early times. Each object on earth or in the sky would thus pass through certain changes, because it chooses so to do; and the progress of science would merely discover the rules which the planets in heaven, or the clouds in the sky, prescribe to themselves in their various motions. It seems almost impossible that such a theory should be seriously revived in these days. It reverses the deep contrast, almost the first-fruits of human experience, perceived alike by the humblest peasant and the wisest philosopher, between unconscious, lifeless matter, and all forms of life, especially those highest in the scale. On this view M. Comte's new "Supreme Being" collective Humanity, is effectually deposed and dethroned; for every atom of the earth, or of the planet Mars, must then far surpass in conscious intelligence the wisest of mankind.

One alternative only seems to remain. The laws of nature must be ascribed to some blind, fatal necessity, by which they exist without a creation and without a beginning, and which prescribes their observance with irresistible power. Such a Fate or Necessity merely substitutes for the God of Christianity another Deity, no less almighty, but without choice, freedom, will, or moral perfections. The conclusion that "the Power which the universe manifests is utterly inscrutable," is supplemented by "laws and causes of evolution, continuity of motion, persistence of force, equivalence of forces, instability of the homogeneous, differentiation, integration, individuality, genesis, hereditary variation, external and internal factors, direct and indirect equilibration." Thus, after shutting out God, as wholly unknowable, from His own universe, we persuade ourselves that we have explained whatever needs explaining, and are fast learning every thing which it can be important for us to know.

This view is applied to the case of astronomy in these words. "Kepler," says Dr. Tyndall, "has deduced his laws from observation. As far back as observation extended, the motions had obeyed these laws, and neither Kepler nor Newton entertained a doubt of their continuing to obey them. Year after year they believed that these laws would illustrate themselves in the heavens. . . . In common with the most ignorant, the scientific man of to-day shows the belief that spring will succeed winter, that summer will succeed spring. But he knows still further, and this knowledge is essential to his intellectual repose, that this succession, besides being permanent, is *necessary*, that the gravitating force exerted between the sun and a revolving sphere *must* produce the observed succession. Not until this relation between forces and phenomena has been established, is the law of reason rendered concentric with the law of nature, and not until then does the mind of the scientific philosopher rest in peace . . . If the force be permanent, the phenomena are *necessary*, whether they resemble or do not resemble any thing that has gone before. Nothing has ever intimated that nature has been crossed by spontaneous action, or that a state of things at any time existed, which could not be rigorously deduced from the preceding state."

The view here ascribed to Newton is the exact reverse of that which his own words, in the Scholium at the close of the "Principia," prove him to have held with the deepest conviction. In his "First Principles," Mr. Spencer makes a statement still more prodigious, that the law of gravitation is not only "deducible mathematically from the relations of space," but is one "of which the negation is inconceivable" and "unthinkable." According to this assertion, Newton's great discovery is not only what every one knew before, but, since its negation is unthinkable, what every one could not help knowing from the beginning of time!

The scientific mind cannot "rest in peace," in a mere perception of likeness and succession among phenomena, but only when they have been traced to "forces, by which an observed succession is produced." So far Dr. Tyndall's remark is true, confirmed by the example of Newton; and is a complete extinction of the Positivist theory, that the true secret of scientific progress is to shut out these metaphysical notions of force and cause, and simply to register phenomena. But when he adds that the same scientific instinct recognizes these forces and their laws as necessary, and appeals to Newton himself in proof, he reverses the clearest facts of history, and the plainest dictates of reason, confirmed by the whole course and constant method of scientific discovery. In the case of gravitation, the statement is in threefold opposition to the certain truth.

First, as to the law itself. It is plain, that Newton, in the "Principia," traces the results of other laws, as equally conceivable; that of force varying as the distance, or constant at all distances, or inversely as the simple distance, the square, and the cube. Also inversely as the $n^{th}$ power; or again, partly as the inverse square, and partly as the distance, in any proportion. In fact these preposterous assertions of Dr. Tyndall and Mr. Spencer would turn almost the whole of the "Principia" into a heap of laborious nonsense. Two-thirds would then be employed in proving what is self-evident, and the remaining third in thinking and reasoning upon what is "unthinkable." Similar reasonings to those of Newton form a main part of nearly every later work on analytical dynamics. Still further, the phenomena of cohesion and of light naturally point to attractive and repulsive forces, varying by laws wholly distinct from the inverse square.

In reality, it is the attempt of these two writers to convert the law of gravitation into a necessary result of the relations of space, which alone is "unthinkable." For this would require us to believe, (1.) a fixed absolute quantum of central force; (2.) its equal transmission to all concentric spherical surfaces, whatever their distance; (3.) its equable distribution over that surface, whatever the variations in the density of the adjacent matter; (4.) its equal exercise and exhaustion on the matter and its pores or interstices, that is, on matter and mere empty space. But a constantly equal density of matter every where, while in continual motion, and an equal action of material forces on matter and on empty space, are strictly inconceivable. What is called necessary and self-evident is not evident at all, and only necessary in this sense, that it necessarily involves a double self-contradiction.

But the law is plainly contingent, not necessary, with reference to matter as acting, and acted on in turn. Since the force varies as the inverse square of the distance, this requires in each atom a centre of force, a point from which the distance is measured. Such centres of force, we are told eight pages before, are unthinkable; though they are the necessary conditions of a law the negation of which is also said to be unthinkable, and have been thought upon and reasoned upon, with definite and demonstrable results, by every analyst from Newton until now. But the position of these centres, far from being necessary, is ever varying from the action of the law itself. We cannot by any effort conceive it as necessary, but rather as capable of an immense variety of alternatives, equally possible. This is true with reference to each atom, as an agent moving other atoms, and as moved by them in its turn.

Let us make this clearer by a little further detail in reference to the medium of light, supposing its elasticity due to repulsive central forces, whether varying as the inverse square of the distance, or by some higher power. The atoms of ether in a linear inch, from the rays and waves of light, are probably not less than a billion. The nearest fixed star is distant more than a trillion of inches. Supposing the distance from which light travels to be more than 3000 times greater, the lineal number of the ethereal atoms will be upwards of $10^{33\frac{1}{3}}$, and their total number above $10^{100}$, or unity followed by a hundred ciphers. The distances of each pair of atoms, on which the repulsive forces depend, will thus equal or exceed $10^{200}$. But the place of each atom is fixed by reference to three co-ordinates. As the radius of the supposed universe, in inches, has at least 33 figures, let us suppose the accuracy of place fixed only to 67 decimals. The number of possible positions for each atom would thus be $10^{300}$, and for all the atoms $10^{400}$; the number of actual distances of one atom from another more than half of $10^{200}$, and of possible distances more than half of $10^{800}$. So that while the actual sets of forces, on which the motions depend, are immensely complex, their number amounting to ten thousand millions multiplied into itself twenty times, the possibilities out of which they are chosen, and which we necessarily conceive, in a physical sense, to be equally possible, exceed this vast number in the proportion of a million multiplied into itself a hundred times, to unity. And this number, so inconceivably vast, must be multiplied further by the number of possible laws of force, to express the amount of demonstrable contingency in that system of forces, which these philosophers gravely reprove the Christian clergy for not receiving submissively, on their own bare *ipse dixit*, as uncontingent, necessary truths!

This notion that laws of nature, discovered slowly by a process of laborious observation, experiment, and induction, when once discovered convey instinctively a sense of their own necessary existence, is itself one of the most gross and palpable of scientific errors. First, it destroys the wide and deep contrast between pure and abstract sciences, of number, space, and hypothetical reasoning, and concrete sciences, which rest on direct evidence, and deal with concrete realities. Next, it stultifies the whole course of experimental science, as laborious trifling, which seeks to obtain *à posteriori* conclusions that might be deduced at once by *à priori* reasoning. Thirdly, it reverses the plainest facts in the history of discovery, which prove that other laws than those now ascertained to exist are equally conceivable, and have been very widely conceived as actual, or reasoned upon as possible. Fourthly, it annuls that process which is the essence of scientific advance, the deduction of results from several possible hypotheses, and their comparison with the observed facts, so as by exclusion to decide which of these possible hypotheses is actually true. Fifthly, it contradicts features of the problem, just as inseparable from it as three dimensions from our conception of space. Thus the first law of Kepler is a consequence of the law of gravitation, which prescribes an ellipse for the form of a planetary orbit. But such an ellipse, in actual astronomy, requires six conditions, the major axis, the excentricity, the inclination, the place of the node, the perihelion place, and the epoch, or place of the planet at a given time. Now the contingency, and possible variety of these six conditions, is just as essential a law of really scientific thought as the necessary character of the equality between the square of the hypothenuse, and the two squares on the sides of a right-angled triangle. It is strange indeed for an experimental philosopher to pronounce a sentence on all the Christian clergy, forbidding them to meddle with physical nature as a field too hard and high for them, unless they will copy his own example in renouncing a truth, which forms almost the first letter in the alphabet of all genuine science.

Scientific unbelief may thus assume either

of two forms, contradicting and excluding each other, yet each of them equally pretentious, and equally false on the side of science, while equally opposed to the truth of God. First, M. Comte renounces forces altogether as metaphysical follies; and then would replace them by laws which are equally metaphysical, and, unless they are laws of force, have no sense or meaning whatever. Next, Dr. Tyndall enjoins the research of forces, as the very first condition of real science; and then ascribes to these forces a necessary existence, disproved by every step in that process of induction, which consists in detecting out of a thousand possibles the actual and the true. It is further disproved by that essential contrast between the geometrical relations of space, and the variable position of material atoms, which it is the first business of the scientific instinct to bring into full relief, and place in the clearest light. From these idle dreams let us turn to the noble words of that philosopher, to whom physical science owes the greatest single step in advance it has ever made, and which form his own moral at the close of his immortal work.

"This most beautiful system of the sun, planets, and comets, could only proceed from the counsel and dominion of an intelligent and powerful Being. And if the fixed stars are the centres of other like systems, these, being formed by the like wise counsel, must all be subject to the dominion of One; especially since the light of the fixed stars and sun is of the same nature, and passes from one into all the systems.

"This Being governs all things, not as the soul of the world, but as Lord over all. The Supreme God is the Being eternal, infinite, absolutely perfect; but a Being, however perfect, without dominion, cannot be said to be Lord God. It is the dominion of a Spiritual Being which constitutes a God; a true, supreme, or imaginary dominion makes a true, supreme, or imaginary God. From His true dominion it follows that the true God is a living, intelligent, powerful Being; and from His other perfections, that He is Supreme or Most Perfect. He is Eternal and Infinite, Omniscient and Omnipotent; that is, His duration is from eternity to eternity, His presence from infinity to infinity; He governs all things, and knows all things that are or can be done. . . . We know Him only by His most wise and excellent contrivances of things, and final causes; we admire Him for His perfections; but we reverence and adore Him on account of His dominion. For we adore Him as His servants; and a God without dominion, providence, and final causes, is nothing else but Fate and Nature. Blind, metaphysical necessity, which is certainly the same always and every where, could produce no variety of things. All that diversity of natural things which we find, suited to different places and times, could come from nothing but the ideas and will of a Being existing necessarily. By way of allegory, God is said to see, to speak, to laugh, to love, to hate, to desire, to give, to receive, to rejoice, to be angry, to work, to build. For our notions of God are taken from the ways of mankind by a certain similitude, which, though not perfect, has however some likeness. And thus much concerning God, to discourse of whom from the appearances of things does certainly belong to Natural Philosophy."

These grave, thoughtful, and pious words of Newton, the first of modern physical philosophers, are a striking contrast to the self-contradicting crudities which some would foist upon the ignorant under the name of scientific truths. All nature, from the lowest atom upward to man, its earthly top-stone, bears witness to the power and greatness of the Supreme Creator, whenever the brutish stage of debasement comes to an end, and the soul of man, ceasing to look only downward and graze with the beasts of the field, lifts up its eyes to heaven. Then only, like Nebuchadnezzar, its understanding returns to it once more, and it learns to bless the Most High, and to praise and honour Him who liveth for ever and ever.

## CHAPTER VIII.

#### ON CREATION AND LIFE.

Life, in all its countless forms, is far more complex, mysterious, and wonderful, than lifeless matter. We look upon the world around us, and see on every side an immense variety of living things, gifted with certain powers of growth, assimilation, reproduction, and, in the animal world, of spontaneous motion, which create an irresistible impression of something that lives and grows or moves, and is a contrast to the inanimate substances which form the rest of the visible and sensible universe. The more we study them, the plainer are the marks in each of some plan or design, adapting each to fulfil some especial mode of being. No piece of human mechanism contains adjustments so various and manifold, so adapted to secure their special objects, as those which can be traced in the structure of plants, and still more in the senses and limbs of animals, growing more complex and various as we rise higher in the scale, till they reach their height in the senses and faculties of living men. And thus the first and simplest induction of science, derived from observation, direct or indirect, of thousands of millions of human beings, and millions of millions, perhaps even trillions, of plants and animals, of a thousand different kinds, is that the world has a Creator and Lord, whose power is great, and His wisdom infinite; and that, as far as the light of the sun surpasses the feeblest taper, so far does His Divine wisdom, who planted the ear and formed the eye, and formed all these countless creatures, gifting them with a life so wonderful, outpass the highest attainments of human reason; so that all the science and skill of man is but a drop, compared to this immeasurable ocean of knowledge, wisdom, and goodness, without limit and without end.

But this first induction of science is followed by another, which, without reversing it, forms with it a partial contrast, and moulds the conception into a new and still more surprising form. For we do not find that each plant and animal springs directly into being before our eyes, possessed of its perfect structure, as by some immediate work of divine and creative power. On the contrary we find, in every case, that they grow up and are born from preexistent and parent forms. This succession, in each kind, is distinct, though extremely various in the methods by which it is accomplished; but the law prevails through the whole extent both of the animal and vegetable world. Instead of these innumerable organisms, rich with the marks of design and secret intelligence and purpose, resulting from innumerable daily repeated acts of direct creation before our eyes, no such acts are ever witnessed; and our thoughts are carried backward to some remote origin, through a line of many successive generations. The idea of creative power in present exercise, day by day, to produce these complicated living machines, with their marvellous internal and external adaptations, is replaced by the need of travelling back to some distant period, when there was not merely a creation of plants and animals of like structure, but also their endowment with strange and mysterious powers to give birth to other individuals, like themselves in plan and structure, through a long and almost unlimited series of successive generations. But the idea of creation itself is only confirmed, and enriched with a deeper element of mystery, while removed beyond the reach of present observation. For, in the first place, a series of past successive generations strictly infinite, is inconceivable, and we feel that a beginning there must have been. And next, the very law of reproduction, by which individuals are multiplied, points naturally to a time when there existed only a single pair, or a few pairs at the most, from which the present numbers might have grown by a law which is seen in constant and hourly operation. And thus the fundamental law of reason, and the special induction from the facts of multiplying life around us, point alike to a beginning; when parent individuals, in each species, were gifted with those wonderful powers which have led to the countless births of later generations.

A third induction, almost or altogether as wide as the two others, binds together their seeming contrast in the unity of one convergent and harmonious theory. For all experience and observation, through all the known history of mankind, and in millions on millions of cases, daily and hourly observed, prove that generation and reproduction, both in plants and animals, is limited to its own kind, and is never seen to travel from one known species to another. It is true that, in the lowest forms of animal life, a class of cases have been discovered of periodic reproduction, where the likeness to the parent type, disguised for a time, only re-appears in the second, third, or fourth generation. But this modification of the simpler law, instead of impairing its force, seems only to confirm it still more clearly; as elliptic cometary orbits confirm the law of periodic revolution, which is seen in the nearly circular orbits of the planets. The gift of reproductive power, as thus fixed by a large induction from millions and billions of examples is not indefinite; and the parent plant or animal has been gifted with a power, not to produce life of any kind whatever, but only a life resembling its own, and differenced by contrast from other forms, which make up the system of the living universe. Thus the marvellous wisdom of every living structure, their immense multitude and variety, prove the existence of an All-wise Creator. The facts of reproduction throw back this creation beyond the time of human experience into the region of faith, and add to it the further element that powers of life and parentage were created and bestowed together. The facts of limited reproduction, of plant by plant, and animal by animal, and man by man, and each in its own kind, fixes on the original creation a double character—of extreme simplicity, in contrast with the countless individuals now in being, but of variety and multiformity, in contrast with some imaginary protoplasm, or wholly indefinite, undivided power of life. It must have been the creation of species and races, not of separate individuals one by one; but of many species and races, each with its own definite powers and mutual relations to the rest, so as to form one various, complex, but marvellously adjusted κόσμος of the vegetable and animal world, with man as the head, leader, and crown of the whole.

A fourth main principle is confirmed by all the inductive research of modern science, and based on the instincts of mankind for thousands of years. There is an ascending scale of being, from inorganic matter, through various forms of life, to man, the crown and top-stone of our terrestrial universe. Life is higher in its lower forms than lifeless matter, animals than plants, beasts and birds than insects and worms; while man, endowed with reason, is higher and nobler in his capacities than all the rest. It may not be possible, indeed, to combine all in one linear series. The truer arrangement may be in cycles, returning into each other, with points of contact alone. But still in reference to the chief varieties of minerals, plants, and animals, by which our earth is adorned and peopled, the ascending steps are clear. All attempts, from anatomical resemblances, to identify men with animals, only furnish new illustrations of the barrier which parts them, and the immense distance that lies between. For who can imagine a conclave of apes or monkies devising laws of biology, and explaining to their friends how, in the course of long ages, while the earth was cooling by laws of radiation, the larvæ of Ascidians had availed themselves of favourable conditions for higher existence, and slowly and steadily developed themselves upward into the monkey form?

There seems to be a fifth conclusion which results, by natural and probable inference, from a scientific review of the broad, well-known facts of human history. Man, as all experience proves, is a social being, with power to acquire, transmit, and communicate knowledge from generation to generation. The strong instinct, which prompts him to leave memorials behind him, extends even to savage tribes. Now the known history of mankind, excluding a few chapters only of Genesis, mounts upward very little more at the highest, than four thousand years. The whole race, also, might have been derived from a single pair in less than five centuries, by a rate of increase actually attained in some families. Even with the very moderate increase of one-twentieth every twenty years, a rate now exceeded in our own and other countries, the whole interval for growth from one pair to the actual number is less than nine thousand years. The existence of such a race, constructive, social, communicative, desirous in various ways of posthumous fame and memory, and its leaving scarce a perceptible trace behind it for millions of years, or even for ten or five thousand years, must be, on purely scientific grounds, almost incredible. The negative inference is so weighty and forcible, as to need nothing less than full and plain counter-evidence to overcome; that the entrance of man on our planet, while not less remote than five, is probably not more remote than ten thousand years.

These wide and large inductions of science with regard to the origin of living creatures, agree fully and entirely with the first chapter of that Book which Jews and Christians, for three thousand years, have received with reverence as the great Creator's own message to mankind. They confirm the earliest declarations of the Bible, and are confirmed by them in their turn. For we are there plainly taught that the universe had a beginning, so that time past is finite, and not infinite; that creation, at least in its latest acts, has followed an ascending scale, from matter to life, from plants to animals, and from animals to man, alone created in the image of God. It teaches, further, that creation was neither of nebulous, abstract life, developed into species by Divine Providence alone, nor of later individuals of which the birth is referred to that Providence, but of distinct species of plants and animals, endowed from the first with specific characters, and large capacities for later increase; that the creation of man was distinct from that of animals, and latest in time; that mankind are descended from a single man and woman, thus formed by the power of God; and that the date of this event, giving the widest range to the Scripture statements, was somewhere more than five, and less than ten thousand years ago. Thus all the *primâ facie* conclusions of the widest inductions of science, and the most patent lessons of the sacred narrative, in five or six cardinal features, are found in perfect agreement with each other.

The Evolution Theory, propounded of late by some philosophers in the name of advancing science, rests on principles almost the reverse of those named above. The universe, it silently assumes, is without beginning, so that all signs of harmony and order, in the present state of the world, may freely be spread out, by infinitesimal division, over past ages unlimited and innumerable. Again, a few fragments of skeletons, and flint implements, real or supposed, in some of the later geological deposits, combined with a law of geological averages, are viewed as the sufficient proof that man's entrance on our planet must be thrown back myriads, or possibly millions of years. The origin of all actual species, and also of fossil species no less marked by specific distinctions, is referred to some latent power of evolution, by which individual forms of life may travel slowly out of their first type, and transmit the change to a later generation, until it accumulates, through long ages, into an entire transmutation. Man himself is included in the developments of this nebulous life-mist; and his genealogy is traced, first, to some unknown quadrumanous type now long extinct, and more remotely to the larvæ of some ancient ascidian forms. The absence of the intermediate links, either in the fossils, or the actual fauna and flora, is explained by the vast amount of strata that remain unexplored; by the igneous changes through which the lower strata have passed, and by similar causes; while the doctrine of gradual evolution of all species from each other is held to be strongly confirmed by the absence of man and the higher mammalian types through all the earlier stages of geological history.

This doctrine agrees naturally with the creed of direct atheism, which denies the existence of a Creator; and of indirect atheism or Positivism, which leaves the being of God an open question, incapable of being solved, and practically unimportant, and confines all religious truth to the solitary maxim that there is some inscrutable Power of which nothing can ever be known. But the view may also be held along with Nomotheism, or that modified Theism, which reckons all direct, periodic interference of God with the universe an impeachment of His perfect foresight, derogating from His wisdom as the Supreme Artificer. Its disciples maintain that it is unworthy of the Divine Workman to construct the machine of the universe in such a way as to need repeated repairs from His more immediate hand; and that it would be a nobler triumph of wisdom and power to construct it from the first so complete and perfect, in its own latent powers, as to need no corrective or interference whatever. The reasoning would be sound, if we were at liberty to assume that the sole aim of the Creator is to form a wonderful piece of machinery, and not to reveal Himself to intelligent moral creatures, made in His own image. It is a scheme of Providence, which implies that God is only the Supreme Carpenter of the universe, but not the Supreme Lawgiver, the King of kings and Lord of lords. To reveal a more perfect and wonderful mechanical skill and physical foresight, by throwing back every act of creative power to innumerable ages before the birth of man,—to hide Himself wholly from view by the very depth of His engineering skill, and leave mankind nothing within their reach to gaze upon but self-evolving powers of matter alone, might be a wise scheme of providence, if the purpose of God were only to develope a race of self-satisfied atheists. But certainly it is not the likeliest plan to waken the notes of that celestial song from the dwellers upon earth;—"Thou art worthy to receive honour, and glory, and power; for Thou hast created all things, and for Thy pleasure they are, and were created."

The comparison of the Scripture Doctrine of Creation with the modern theory of Evolution is highly difficult, not only from the complexity and vastness of the field of thought to be traversed, but from the obscurity which still rests on the fundamental notions of life and vital power. The accumulation of facts and details, and the store of scientific materials, has here far outstripped, for the present, the progress of clear conceptions and well defined theory. In its place, the Positivists and non-religious students of science present us with an immense variety of new metaphysical and abstract phrases, of the very class which the founder of the school professes to exclude and condemn. In the limits of the present work it will only be possible to make a few preparatory remarks on the false, unscientific assumptions which lie at the root of this Evolution Theory, in its attempted application to explain the origin of all living things.

## CHAPTER IX.

### ON CREATION AND EVOLUTION.

The doctrine of Creation, received by the whole Christian Church, and all Christian philosophers of later times, and confirmed by the testimony of Moses and the Prophets, of Christ and His Apostles, is cast aside with contempt by modern Positivism, and has been denounced in the following terms:—

"The belief in special creations of organisms is a belief that arose among men during the era of profoundest darkness, and belongs to a family of beliefs which have nearly all died out, as enlightenment has increased. It is without a solitary established fact on which to stand, and when the attempt is made to put it into definite shape, it turns out to be only a pseudo-idea. The mere verbal hypothesis, which men idly accept as real or thinkable, is of the same nature as would be one based on a day's observation of human life, that each man or woman was specially created, an hypothesis not suggested by evidence, but by lack of evidence, formulating absolute ignorance into a semblance of positive knowledge. This hypothesis, wholly without support, essentially inconceivable, and thus failing to satisfy men's intellectual need, fails also to satisfy their moral sentiment. It is quite inconsistent with those conceptions of the divine nature which they profess to entertain. If infinite power was to be demonstrated, then either by the special creation of individuals, or the production of species after a method akin to that of individuals, it would be better demonstrated than by the two methods the hypothesis assumes to be necessary. If infinite goodness was to be demonstrated, not only do the provisions of organic structure, if specially devised, fail to demonstrate it, but there is an enormous mass of them which imply malevolence rather than benevolence."

"Thus the hypothesis of special creations turns out to be worthless; worthless by its derivation, worthless in its intrinsic incoherence, worthless as absolutely without evidence, worthless as not supplying an intellectual need, worthless as not satisfying a moral want." (Spencer, Princ. Biol. p. 344.)

The modesty of these assertions needs no remark. The one question of importance is their truth or falsehood. There are eight counts in this indictment against the truth of Scripture and the faith of all Christians. The first is that the doctrine is "worthless in its origin," being of early date, and arose "during the era of profoundest darkness." Being a primitive hypothesis, it is probably untrue. If interpretations of nature by aboriginal men were erroneous in other directions, they were most likely erroneous in this also.

The doctrine of a creation is thus rejected as the supposed creed of supposed "aboriginal men." According to Positivist theories, these had been struggling upwards for myriads of years before Adam, and lived therefore in "the era of profoundest darkness." Christian believers in general wholly deny the existence of these aboriginal savages. They do not admit that doubtful and vague inferences from a few flints and fragments of bones, depending on many obscure and uncertain elements, can outweigh the direct testimony of the Word of God, and the indirect conclusion, strongly adverse to pre-Adamic generations, from the limits of known human history. But let us grant that they existed, still we have no grain of direct evidence as to their theories of creation. By the hypothesis of Positivism, however, their creed was simple Fetichism, which seats a divine energy in every creature, and so turns it into an object of worship. Such a creed is almost the same with the doctrine of evolution; and is an entire contrast to the doctrine of Scripture, or the creation of plants and animals, once for all, by the Supreme and Almighty God. The argument, besides the double falsehood of its main assertion, involves a third fallacy, for all early beliefs are not untrue.

Let us turn from these mere fictions to the known facts of history. The doctrine that God created plants and animals in the beginning, "after their kind," has prevailed for three thousand years, from Moses until now, among the best, noblest, and wisest of men. It has been no crude fancy of ignorant peasants alone. Among its firm believers are all the Prophets and all the Apostles, most of the Greek philosophers, and Christian divines and men of science for fifteen centuries, the intellectual lights and standard-bearers of the leading nations of the earth. It includes among its disciples and adherents nearly all the great names, like Bacon, Kepler, Boyle, and Newton, by whom the chief advances of modern science have been made. Its true birthplace is in no flint-weapon manufactory, or bone-cavern—in an "era of profoundest darkness." It is in thick darkness of a very opposite kind, when Moses, learned in all the wisdom of the Egyptians—the foremost, wisest, and noblest of all living men—drew near to the presence of Jehovah, talked with Him face to face in the holy mount as a man speaketh with his friend, and received from Him those messages which have enlightened and cheered the minds and hearts of sinful men through every later age of the world's history. The rival theory is little more than a modern revival of pagan Fetichism, thrown into a more systematic form. It is an ephemeron unknown to, or rejected by, the great lights of every past age, born yesterday, and ready to expire to-morrow. Its birth was in the thick moral darkness of a French Atheistic Revolution, miscalling itself light, which set quickly in a sea of blood. And it will breathe its last when unbelief has ripened once more into open and daring blasphemy, and the King of Heaven, whom it seeks to thrust far away from human view, shall "arise in majesty to shake terribly the earth."

But the doctrine is said to be one of "a special class of mistaken beliefs," already destroyed by advancing knowledge, and almost the only member of the family that survives among educated people. "Ask any tolerably informed man whether he accepts the cosmogony of the Indians, the Greeks, or the Hebrews, and he will regard the question as next to an insult. The doctrine enters the mind in childhood as one portion of a story which, as a whole, has been long since rejected." It is the last dodo of a species ready to expire.

The actual spread of unbelief, greatly underrated by religious men of sanguine and hopeful temper, is often as greatly exaggerated by sceptics themselves. These remarks are one clear proof. The cosmogony of the Hebrews means, of course, the record of creation in the Book of Genesis; and an old precedent is followed, by holding up the truth of God's Word to contempt and shame between two heathenish mythologies. Is it, then, true that most educated men in our country would count it an insult to be asked whether they still hold the Bible to be a divine revelation? The only insult resented, in very many cases, would be the implied suspicion of their not believing it. In many more the question, if not held to be an insult, would be counted a snare to betray them, by some confession of partial doubt, into odium with firmer believers. The class who would reckon it an insult to be suspected of believing it, and of not rejecting its first portion as a mere Jewish legend, are still, so far as recent tests are a guide, a very small minority both among educated and uneducated men.

The assumption, then, in point of fact, is wholly untrue; but the argument based on this fiction is still more worthless. A time may come, though far from being now arrived, when nine-tenths of educated men in Christendom may wholly renounce their faith in God, in Christ, in the Bible, and, along with these, in the doctrine of Creation. They may possibly come to receive, as their new and nobler creed, the vast self-developing power of polypes and star-fishes, and the larvæ of old Ascidians. They may hold that some of these, more prosperous than the rest in satisfying unknown "conditions of existence," have raised themselves, by the infinite repetition of infinitesimal efforts, more and more above their fellows; until, as "collective humanity," they form M. Comte's new and improved "Supreme Being," and occupy boldly the vacant throne of the Most High. The truth of the unbelieving theory, on Positive principles, may perhaps be lawfully inferred from the number of unbelievers. But on Christian principles no such conclusion follows. There will only be a new proof of the fatal proneness of men to choose idols, and forsake the living God; and a new pledge that the time is at hand when this latest idol of human folly shall be abolished by the bright dawning of the Dayspring from on high. Sceptical theories are rendered more seductive and dangerous when numbers embrace them, but this is no real evidence of their truth. The wide and fatal spread of a pestilence might as reasonably be held to prove that its victims are free from all disease.

The doctrine is charged, further, with a total want of evidence. It is "not countenanced by a single fact." No one ever saw a special creation. Whenever the order of organic nature is exposed to view, it expels this conception, and it survives only in connexion with imagined places, where the order of phenomena is unknown.

The creation of new species continually, in modern times, is nowhere affirmed in the Bible, and is no part of popular Christian faith. Some naturalists may have held it as a private conjecture; but if the proofs of that conjecture have failed, this has not the least bearing on the Scripture doctrine. Any allusion to such a belief may thus be set aside at once, since it can only substitute a false issue for the question really in debate. And this is whether existing species grew, one out of another, at some period immensely remote, by some self-unfolding power of matter and living things, or whether they were formed, each after its own kind, by the immediate power and wisdom of the Living God.

The objection that no one has witnessed a special creation, if honestly made, implies a singular confusion of thought. The question is of the origin of species, which are known to have co-existed with mankind as far back as records of human history extend. Any hypothesis which placed their origin within human observation would thus not only contradict Scripture, but the simplest datum of the scientific problem proposed. Alike on every view, of which the falsehood is not self-evident, the origin of species is before human observation, and beyond the range of direct historic record.

. All the evidence, which alone is possible from the nature of the problem, confirms the doctrine of Creation. First, it is directly affirmed by a divine message, ratified by the lips of Him whose name is the Truth, and whom Christians know to be the Son of God, the Word and Wisdom of the Most High. Next, the known facts of generation lead us back, without miracle, to a time when there were only a few pairs, or a single pair, of each species. But this principle, though confirmed so far by an immense experience, leads us no farther. Reason teaches that there must have been a beginning, and that an infinite series, backward, of single pairs each producing a single pair, is incredible and unnatural, and even impossible. Here reason and faith combine, then, to complete the lesson of experience. They point alike to a beginning, in which first parents of each species received their double powers of life and reproduction direct from the will of a Divine Creator. A consilience of evidence, from distinct sources, thus conspires to prove the same truth.

Let us now compare the evidence for the rival theory. The only direct evidence possible for facts before human record is a Divine testimony. Such a testimony exists, received as divine by the faith of Jews and Christians for more than two thousand years, and sealed as true and genuine by plainly recorded sayings of the Son of God. The theory sets this aside with contempt as an irrational "Hebrew cosmogony," and begins by giving the lie direct to the Saviour and Judge of the world. Next, it replaces the fact, proved by millions or billions of examples, with no single certain exception, that like produces like, and that plants and animals generate, not laterally and indefinitely, but each within defined limits, by a mere conjecture that in earlier ages like often produced the unlike, and deviated into some quite different type of being. Thirdly, it invents, also by conjecture alone, a large number of such unproved mutations, backward to lower, or forward to higher forms of being. After this immense licence of conjecture, with an entire absence of positive facts to confirm or justify them, it leaves the real difficulty just as great as before, and greater still. A creation, immense ages ago, of innumerable monads, able to organize themselves into innumerable polypes, able in their turn to develope themselves in the slow flight of time into Platos, Bacons, and Newtons, requires as great an exertion of divine power as the Scripture narrative, and one ten thousand times more perplexing, mysterious, and inconceivable.

A fourth objection follows. The doctrine of creation "cannot be framed into a coherent thought," is only "a pseud-idea," and "an illegitimate symbolic conception." For the creation of matter is inconceivable, and implies a relation in thought between something and nothing, which is impossible. And next, if what is meant is a rearrangement of existing matter, how can it be? To suppose a myriad supernatural impulses given to as many different atoms, to build the new plant or animal, multiplies rather than solves the mystery. It is a creation of force, and this is as inconceivable as that of matter. The Hebrew idea of clay moulded into the man is too grossly anthropomorphic for modern belief, but what substitute can be proposed more conceivable? The case is one where men do not believe, but only fancy they believe.

This argument is so freely used by this leading advocate of evolution, as to suggest a doubt whether, on his own principles, the later stages of development have not wholly failed, so that men are as incapable of thinking as hydras and sea-anemones to the present day. According to "First Principles" we cannot really think either of a self-existent universe, or a self-developed universe, or a universe created by the power of God. Atheism, Pantheism, and Theism, are all "unthinkable." The creation of matter is inconceivable, the creation of space, its non-creation, its entity, and its non-entity. We cannot think of self-existence no where, and we cannot think of it any where. We cannot think of space as subjective, an objective non-entity, an objective attribute, or an objective entity; as limited or unlimited, as infinitely or not infinitely divisible. We cannot think of matter as continuous and solid, or as solid atoms, indivisible and discontinuous, or as centres of force alone. We cannot think of motion either as absolute or as relative, of force as acting where it is, or where it is not, indirectly through a medium, or directly at a distance, and cannot think of it as ceasing to act, though we cannot think of its action in either of the two ways mentioned, or invent a third way, distinct from either. A new style of scientific controversy seems invented, in which whatever view a speculator dislikes is pronounced at once to be "literally unthinkable."

One grand fallacy runs through all these remarks. Every thing on which men debate and reason, and hold opposite views, is thinkable in a practical sense, or else there could not be this diversity and conflict of judgment. But every complex idea or proposition, which involves real contradiction, is unthinkable in this sense, that when clearly analyzed, the contradiction is brought to light, and some elements of the compound exclude the rest. Again, every subject has fixed relations to the unseen and infinite, which are not comprehensible, although strictly "thinkable," or objects of real and definite thought. We see and know in part, and recognize something that remains unknown. But when the same term "unthinkable" is applied alike to these three distinct notions, as a besom to sweep away obnoxious opinions, the result is a deplorable chaos and confusion. When contradictions, one of which must be true, are affirmed alike to be unthinkable, the word is used in two senses widely different, to denote a true, real, unsearchable mystery, and an unreal, untrue, and impossible contradiction.

Let us turn to the present subject, and take for an example the creation of the first lion and lioness in the popular view. We can easily conceive their sudden appearance before us in Paradise or elsewhere, not having been seen or existed before. Whether the matter of their bodies has been newly created, or brought from other sources, and only organized and endued with new life, hardly increases or lessens the ease of the conception, which in itself is easy and simple. If the cause be asked, the Christian reply is simple, Almighty Power. We conceive such a change to be clearly possible in itself, and thus certainly within the scope of Divine Omnipotence. "He spake, and it was done." If it be asked further, How and by what especial process, did God create these animals? the Christian does not pretend to explain, because it is not revealed. A first beginning, from reason, is certain in one stage or another, and wherever placed, it must be mysterious. The mystery is thinkable, conceivable, but not comprehensible. There is something clear, definite, which we may believe firmly on adequate testimony, and from which, to a certain extent, we may reason clearly. But there is much beyond,—secret things of the Lord God, where reason pauses on the mountain side, or on the mountain top, and gazes on the blue sky above, and where seraphs veil their faces and adore.

But when the admitted mysteriousness of creation is turned into an argument for the rival theory, the answer is plain. The mystery in this doctrine of evolution is just as great,

but with a twofold difference, that it assigns
effects to causes plainly inadequate, and that it
has no germ of direct evidence in its favour, and
even a divine testimony of its utter falsehood.
Let us suppose a polype or oyster in the same
scene as before. This polype or oyster disappears, and suddenly a lion and lioness stand
before us in their stead. Has their presence
lessened the mystery in this sudden appearance
of the nobler animals? Clearly it has given us
two mysteries—an appearance and a disappearance—instead of one only. Let us next
interpose a hundred or a thousand changes, in
the first of which the polype disappears, and
something different comes in its place, and a
third, and a fourth, and a fifth, till after a
hundred or thousand substitutions again a lion
and lioness stand before us. Have we not here
two hundred or two thousand mysteries, of disappearances and new appearances, instead of
one? Now expand the hour into ten thousand
years, and interpolate a hundred embryos and
births in every stage. Wherein is the mystery
lessened? The total change is as great as
before, and the steps interposed, ten thousand
in number, only add fresh elements, each inscrutable, or in the terms of the objection,
unthinkable. Why should twenty thousand

unthinkables be more easy to the thoughts than one only? But a double contrast remains. The creation of this lion and lioness, when referred at once to divine power, is referred to a cause our reason is compelled to own adequate, and more than adequate, to the result. But when we ascribe to a polype or oyster the power to raise itself upward, by slow instalments of one-hundredth per cent., nearer and nearer to a lion, we must either make it different from all actual polypes or oysters, where no such power has been traced, a disguised lion-embryo, lasting for ages; or else we must introduce, broken down into ten thousand fragments, to disguise its own presence, that Divine Almighty Power, which the other doctrine exhibits in its simple and native grandeur without disguise.

The probable speculations of an ephemeron, endued with reason, on the origin of men and women, are conceived to furnish another argument against the doctrine of creation, taught in the Word of God. Such an insect, it is said, would certainly suppose each man and woman separately created, since no appreciable change of structure takes place in them during the few hours to which its observation would extend. But the period over which human records range is said to be ephemeral, compared with the life of a species. Thus there is no reason to suppose the creed of a creation, the first conclusion of mankind, to be nearer the truth than this faulty conclusion of a reasoning ephemeron concerning individual men.

This argument from fairyland against the Christian doctrine of creation is ephemeral in every sense. With the first breath of deeper reflection its insect life disappears. It rests on six or seven assumptions, all equally groundless; that reasoning ephemera, being wiser than philosophers and divines, would all reason in one way, and reach the same conclusion; that their reasonings on a higher and more permanent race, not on their own, are parallel to man's reasonings on himself and a thousand inferior and more short-lived races; that the experience of an individual insect is parallel to the cumulative knowledge of a hundred generations of mankind; that ten thousand species, only known to us as co-existing with man for some thousands of years, may be assumed, without evidence, to have lasted twenty thousand times longer than he; that the life of a species, which has no apparent limit but foreign violence, answers strictly to the life of an individual, which has laws fixed by a large experience;

that the supposed inference is faulty in its Christian part, which is sound and true, and not in that conjectural addition which resembles the doctrine of evolution; and lastly, that the sceptic philosopher has a larger experience to build on than the Christian believer, in the same ratio as man's life exceeds that of the insect ephemeron. All these seven bases of the objection are equally untrue, but it will be enough to consider the first and sixth alone.

Now if analogy from the possible reasonings of ephemera are to be our guide, we are bound to compare three varieties of insect philosophy. One ephemeron shall be a prosaic Atheist, the second a poetic Evolutionist, the third a simple and sober Theist. The first observes no change in men or women in his brief lifetime, and never reasons upward that there must be some great First Cause. So he adopts the simplest and dullest form of Atheism, that each man and woman he sees is uncreated and eternal, and has existed just as he sees them through millions and billions of ephemeral lifetimes, backward without end. The poetic Evolutionist rejects equally any First Cause and any beginning, but is more aspiring in his conjectures about events long before he was born. He simplifies the complex phenomena that meet his philosophic mind, by supposing that men and women are ephemera that have lost their wings, and in long process of time, and after ten thousand generations, each increasing in length one single day, have slowly attained their actual form and superior stability. They are thus, in his enlightened creed, happy, prosperous, independent developments, from remote ancestors of his own; so that a race of self-created ephemera, slowly and surely developing into men and women, are the true original of the universe. The third ephemeron, a sober Theist, would reason differently. By direct observation of men and women he will infer, either absence of change, or changes slow and gradual compared with his own. Comparing their intelligence with his own consciousness of reasoning powers, he would see that they differed in degree, not in kind, and would gain a probable inference that they had successive generations, only of longer period, like his own. This idea, however, from want of experience and direct evidence, he will leave a doubtful and open question. But, being reasonable, he will infer that neither himself nor his ephemeral parents, nor these men and women, nor their parents, if such there were, could be a multiple origin to themselves; that there must be a higher First Cause, and that either these men, or else their first parents, like the first parents of his own short-lived race, had been created by this Unseen Power. This conclusion of the Theist among ephemera would be true, agreeing with all the evidence in his reach, and limited by it. The two other conclusions, of the prosaic and poetic Atheists, would be divergent falsehoods, uniting contradictory guesses on details beyond their experience with the common denial of a truth which, as endued with reason, they ought to have perceived and known. And if they had received a message from the Creator on the order of creation, and refused it on the ground that several hours' experience proved men and women to undergo no change at all, but to have lived on from all eternity, or that some minutes of philosophical thought made them confident that they were only ephemera which had lost their wings, and grown slowly and immensely in size, they would then be a true counterpart to the Atheism and Positivism of our own times.

But if divine power is to be shown by the creation of species, would it not be still better displayed by the creation of individuals? Why this process of natural generation? Why not prove omnipotence more fully by the supernatural production of plants and animals from hour to hour? Are we to say that the Creator could form individuals in this way, but not species? This would assign a limit to His power, instead of magnifying it. To say that it was not possible is suicidal in a Theist. But if possible, what end is served by the special creation of species, that would not be better served by that of individuals? To what purpose could be the supposed signs of divine power, when there were no beings to contemplate them? Either we must say that species could not be formed like individuals, which denies omnipotence, or else there would have been superfluous exercises of power, to no reasonable end.

Here the first reply is very simple. This special creation, at a certain period, of plants and animals after their kind, is not received by Christians from their *à priori* reasonings alone. They put faith in a divine testimony. They hold this to be clearly taught in a message which, on external and internal evidence, they accept as sent from the Living God. They make no compact with their Maker, that they will believe nothing He tells them that He has done, unless He first explains to their full satisfaction all the reasons why it was done. Others may account such a rule wise philosophy; they account it nothing better than profaneness and folly. They cannot receive the two maxims peacefully side by side, that "the Power the universe manifests is utterly inscrutable," so that of the acts of this great Being, and their reasons, nothing whatever can possibly be known; and still that He is so entirely sub-human that our knowledge by revelation of a single divine act involves, of course, our perfect competence to expound all the reasons why it was done. They hold the middle pathway of Scripture and of reason between these violent extremes; that God is the Father of lights, who has revealed Himself to men, and of whom much may and ought to be known; and still that His judgments are unsearchable, and His ways past finding out, though fuller insight is promised to the lowly and obedient in the life to come.

The objection assumes, further, that this derivation of species from each other, like individuals, is possible in itself without fresh acts of divine power. But this is unproved; and till we know the nature and laws of life more clearly, seems unprovable. With tenfold more warrant than in the case of centres of force, we may hold this to be a pseud-idea, "a symbolic conception of the illegitimate order," and unthinkable. The power to aim at a special type of organized being, and on reaching it, to produce other individuals, aiming at the same type, may be the definition of animal life in all its forms. If so, a power wholly to desert that type, and aim at another quite distinct, would annul the first definition, and would replace the being first defined by another, having no existence before. This view seems highly probable, but at least the contrary is not self-evident. It may thus be no real limiting of divine power, to say that species cannot be generated like individuals without new acts of creation, any more than to say that a square cannot generate a sphere by its revolution, as a point may generate a circle, or a circle a sphere. And thus the whole objection may be simply a chimera, which clearer insight into the true nature of life would banish into the limbo of "illegitimate conceptions" and impossible dreams.

But even if the generation of species be possible in its own nature, the objection is rash and groundless; and the plan of creation, taught in the Bible, may be shown to satisfy the great ends of Divine Providence in the highest degree. The argument is now transferred from the low marshes of Positivism to the high ground of Christian Theism. The objector, professing total ignorance of the inscrutable Power that governs the universe, maintains that, on the maxims of Theists themselves, he can prove the creation of species to be the worst alternative. Now the first maxim of Christian Theism is that the design of creation is to glorify the great Creator by the wonderful works of His hands. This end must be secured, in the largest degree, by every increase in the fulness and variety of the gifts He bestows; but subject to this one condition, that the mode of their bestowment shall not wholly conceal their true source, and make it easy and natural to rest in second causes, and ascribe to them an origin independent of the Creator's will and good pleasure. The creation of plants and animals, with an imparted power to increase and multiply in successive generations without limit, plainly magnifies the power, wisdom, and foresight of the Creator in a very high degree. The gift of parentage, in every case, amplifies and redoubles the simpler gift of being. Nor is this the only gain. That scheme of nature, over which man is gifted with sovereignty and large control, is vastly extended, compared with a constant creation of individual plants and animals, by which all the higher arts of human life would at once expire. Human existence is enriched and ennobled by various ties of race, brotherhood, conjugal and parental love, and filial honour and obedience, far beyond what a scheme of mere individualism could attain. At the same time, the constant law that like produces its like only, compels the reason to travel upward, in a thousand distinct lines, to the common origin of these various species, and there to recognize the Divine hand which at the first called them into being, and gifted them with powers so wonderful and strange. Faith in creation is ennobled by its transfer from the field of transient phenomena and momentary novelties of experience to calm and sure inferences of reason on the vast outlines of Providence, and on the laws observed, for thousands of years, by millions on millions of individuals, in ten thousand races of diverse powers, crowned by the history of man himself, the prince and sovereign of these lower works of God.

Let us now compare the moral results of the other alternative. All species on this view, may be seen, by careful observation, slowly melting into each other. The numbers of each kind cease to supply any guess, however rude, as to the time of its remote origin. In the eye of science, it ceases to be a kind at all, a class of perfectly formed individuals, born from others as perfect, and bearing witness, in each descent, to the skill of the great Creator. They become a small number of happy accidents, surviving from a much larger number of unfortunate misadventures, which have perished and disappeared. The tendency, in going backward, is only to lose higher forms in the lower, the few in the many, the distinct and fully organized in the dim and obscure, and the further we recede, the more confused, chaotic and unmeaning is the spectacle that lies before us. What result must naturally follow? The glorious vision of a wise, intelligent Creator is lost wholly in a nebulous mist, removed so far back into an immeasurable past, and there made so obscure and unaccountable in the mode of His action, as practically to be blotted out entirely from human view. And what will be left in its place? Some vague, doubtful, blind admission of some inscrutable Power, of which the motives and modes of action are utterly inaccessible and unknown, and a vision of trillions on trillions of animalcules, inconceivably small, existing in ages inconceivably remote, no one knows why or how, and slowly working their way upward, by some lucky combination of chances, or some mysterious fate and power of self-development, into nobler and higher forms. The Living God is dethroned and annihilated in the thoughts of men, and there will be enthroned in His stead a mystery beyond all the mysteries of Christian faith, a sublime maggot theory of the universe!

Such, almost literally at the present hour, is the incipient moral effect of this new theory of development. Among its votaries may be a few Nomotheists, with some abstract faith in a Creator who creates only by law, and who, at some time infinitely remote, imparted once for all to living monads a power of indefinite ascent in the scale of being, which the Theist cannot explain or understand. Most of them, however are either Atheists, who affirm that " there is no God," or Nihilists, who hold a creed practically equivalent, that of the Unseen Power which the universe manifests nothing can ever be known. In theory there is a distinction between the three alternatives, but in practice it disappears. The doctrine of Creation, revealed in the Bible, has upheld alone, for three thousand years, in the hearts of millions on millions, habits of faith, and reverence, and holy worship, towards the Supreme Lord and Governor of the universe. The rival theory is not eighty years old, and in its calendar of feasts to Moses and Cæsar, Frederic and Bichat, and its votive rites to dead women who on its own theory have ceased to exist, the grey hairs of dotage are already upon it. Far from tending to magnify the glory and greatness of the Creator, the theory, by the confession and practice of those who obtrude on its adversaries this preposterous plea in its favour, tends to thrust them far away beyond even the telescopic vision of ordinary men. Its moral tendencies, and even its actual results, as tested by its ephemeral experience, can be most fully described by the words of the patriarch more than three thousand years ago :—" Which say unto God, 'Depart from us, for we desire not the knowledge of Thy ways.'"

The doctrine of special creation is said, further, to involve hopeless theological difficulties. The assumption involves the consequence, that the designer intended every thing that results from the design. Why, then, during millions of years did there exist on the earth no beings endowed with capacities for wide thought and high feeling? What must we think of the pain-inflicting appliances and instincts with which animals are endowed? From the earliest periods of geology there has been going on a universal carnage. Fossil as well as living structures show us elaborate weapons for destroying other animals. There has been a perpetual preying of the superior on the inferior, the devouring of the weak by the strong. On the hypothesis of special creation, there must either have been a deliberate intention to produce these results, or inability to prevent them. Which alternative are we to prefer? What shall we further say of the numerous species of parasites, of inferior forms destroying the superior, and elaborate appliances for the prosperity of organisms incapable of feeling, at the expense of misery to organisms capable of happiness? An enormous mass of the provisions of organic structure, it is affirmed, "imply malevolence rather than benevolence."

There is one gain, at least, in this crowning objection to the Scripture doctrine of Creation. The true issue involved is brought at length into clear relief. All Nomotheistic compromises, and saving phrases of " creation only by law " are set aside. The argument is aimed, not against the notions of caprice, uncertainty, and defect of foresight, ascribed rashly to separate creative acts, but against all wisdom, goodness, and holiness in the Creator, whatever the mode and order of creation may be. It is the old objection of the "dull, complaining Atheist," that the world seems "oddly made, and every thing amiss," cast hastily into a modern mould, to uproot all faith in Divine Providence from the minds of men. Thousands of such attempts have been made before. This is only the latest effort, in the name of progressive science, to restore the reign of Chaos and blind Chance and Fate in the moral world.

It would require a volume to reply fully to an objection so wide in its range, and so disastrous, if once accepted as valid and true, in its bearing on the moral destinies of all mankind. I must content myself here with a few remarks only, that will suggest a fuller answer to thoughtful minds.

And first, it is easy to exaggerate the sufferings of the lower creatures in that process of the life of some sustained by the death of others, which prevails widely in the animal world. The ascription of the poet to "the poor beetle that we tread upon" of as great a suffering "as when a giant dies," does violence to all the analogies of nature, and may safely be reckoned wholly untrue. The dignity of the form of life measures the loss, and probably too, the pain, when it is parted with and comes to an end. The fear of death and the pain of dying are most developed in forms of life which approach nearest to the human, since the structure is more developed, the powers are wider and more various, and the life conveys a higher pleasure. And thus, in spite of this mystery of perpetual death, and even violent death, there is clearly among the lower animals a vast overplus on the side of enjoyment. There is no provision in nature, except in some forms of disease, for prolonged, protracted torture. The pain of dying in animals arises mainly from the preciousness of the life that is torn away. But the death is of moments or minutes, the life enjoyed is of days, or months, or years. In men the fear of coming evil may pain as much as present calamity; but among animals this source of suffering has a far narrower range, and can be traced in a few higher kinds alone. So that the spontaneous instinct of all unbiassed observers is that the animal creation, in spite of its mysteries, while it lies in the penumbra of the dark shadow of moral evil in the higher world above it, still bears witness in every part to the Creator's goodness.

Again, the doctrine of Creation, as revealed in Scripture, is only the first page of a larger and fuller message, which includes a foreseen entrance of moral evil, with a long train of attendant sufferings and sorrows. We are plainly taught that the whole economy of God's providence, here below, would comprise long ages of moral warfare, and that cloud and darkness would prepare the way for the final victory of the Divine goodness. The lower creation, it is also revealed, were framed with reference to the high ends of God's moral dominion. It is no complete whole in itself, but was made subject to vanity through the sin of man. The objection omits the human race, and limits itself to the lower creatures only. But Christian theology does not accept the artificial limitation. For while the overplus of enjoyment in all animal life may suffice to vindicate the Divine goodness from the charge of malevolence, the variety and extent of the seeming drawbacks and contrasts is referred constantly, in Scripture, to the presence and spread of moral evil.

The objection drawn from the many kinds of parasitic life, with the resulting growth of humbling and painful, and even dangerous diseases, is removed by this higher view of God's universal providence, and by this alone. The chief allusions to the subject in Scripture are found in connexion with the plagues of Egypt, or the threatenings on the chosen people for their relapses into vice and heathen idolatry. The same class of facts are alluded to by the patriarch in his affliction: "My flesh is clothed with worms, and clods of dust. My skin is broken, and become loathsome." "I have said to corruption, Thou art my father; to the worm, Thou art my mother and my sister." The haughty Herod, in the hour of his blasphemous pride, "was eaten of worms, and gave up the ghost." We need, then, no subtle physiological inquiry into the origin and nature of parasitic races, to look upon them as the results, not of health, but of disease; and in the case of mankind, to view them as signs that a first and higher state has been lost, and man himself, like the lower creatures, has in different ways been "made subject to vanity.".

When once these higher truths of Scripture have been received, and their consequences and bearings fully considered, all the difficulties which have been started from the more repulsive facts of animal physiology, disappear, or become fresh witnesses for the truth of revelation. The seeming discord is replaced by the tones of a deeper harmony, and the partial evil, in a fuller sense than Pope or Bolingbroke might understand, ministers to "universal good," and reveals more brightly the glory of the Divine Creator. It is not likely that those who hold Theology to be an impossible science, and with whom "the Unknowable" is the only title of the living God, should do more than stumble at the threshold of the temple, and when they have raised a cloud of theological difficulties, grope on in thick darkness. But when the discernment of positive philosophers is baffled and perplexed by the number of human parasites, the Bothriocephalus and Tænia, the Trichocephalus, the Trichina and Leptothrix, as the magicians of old were baffled by the flies and lice in Egypt, believers in the word of God have "light in their dwellings." The various objections, confidently brought against the revealed doctrine of creation, only recoil upon their authors, to prove that, in renouncing a Moral Governor of the world, they renounce all faculty of true insight into the deeper mysteries of providence, that the highest and noblest walk of human thought, which deals with the spiritual aspect of man's nature, and the ways, the works, and moral perfections of the Most High.

## CHAPTER X.

### EVOLUTION, AS AN INDUCTIVE THEORY.

ALL Science depends on a double process of induction and deduction. The first arranges and classifies phenomena, and thus attains to certain empirical laws, which embody the results of past observation in their most comprehensive form. The second traces the results of some probable or possible hypothesis, to decide on its agreement or disagreement with these results. In case of agreement, it is assumed to be true, and its further consequences are then traced, to supply new confirmations of its truth, and anticipate the results of new and varied experiments.

The theory, which would explain the origin and nature of all organic life, apart from any acts of creative power, by a process of evolution, must thus be open to a double test. Does it fulfil the claims of sound, philosophical induction, and sum up correctly the results of actual observation on the largest scale? Does it conform to the rules of deductive science, start from clear axioms and definite laws, and trace out consequences in such a way as to admit of being tested by new observations? In the present work an answer will be given to the former question alone. The other calls for a more expanded reply.

The nature, origin, and mutual relations, of existing plants and animals, and still further, of all the extinct species and remains of geology, is the problem which calls for solution. On the side of science, its difficulty is plainly very great. The times of which the history is sought are thousands, or even myriads or millions of years remote, before the actual or possible date of human records. The physical inquiry alone is a million times more complex than that which has fully tested the resources of analysis, and the zeal of astronomers, for three centuries from Kepler until now. The question is not of the motion of a few separate spheres under one simple law of gravitation, but of the past condition, thousands of years ago, of the ever-shifting wastes of land, water, air, rock, and sand, earth, ocean, and river, which compose the part of our planet accessible to man, under complex laws of gravitation, cohesion, chemical affinity, heat, and electricity, dependent in their turn on the general state of the solar system.

And the problem, as one of physiology, is more difficult still, since it depends on higher laws of organism and life, of which little is clearly known. Its aim is to determine the genesis of half a million species of plants and animals, and billions of individuals, in thousands of generations, under varying conditions; when the birth of a single primrose or violet, a polype or trilobite, is beyond the power of actual science to explain clearly, and no single law of vital action has passed from the empirical into the scientific stage. In dealing with a problem so vast, with knowledge so microscopic and imperfect, extreme modesty and caution must be the first instinct of genuine science. If loose guesses and ingenious fancies replace the process of strict induction, and verbal and metaphysical generalizations are mistaken for definite and deductive reasoning from scientific laws of force or vital action, the results can only be disastrous; in science, confusion of thought, and a practical failure; and in morals possibly still worse, a blind, Titanic assault on the very foundations of natural and revealed religion.

In dealing with so vast a problem, and periods so remote, the first instinct of genuine science must be to welcome eagerly any grain of direct evidence, if such can be found. The known records of human observations go back only four thousand years, and for the first of these are vague and scanty in the extreme. But the problem attempts to reach backward for myriads of years, even before the time when man was seen upon the earth. Reason teaches plainly that there must have been a beginning, and a Divine Beginner, by whom all things consist. The only direct evidence available for these early times must be a message from the Creator to mankind. Such a message, according to the constant faith of the Jewish nation and the Christian Church for three thousand years, has really been given to man, and begins with a brief and clear statement of the order and method of man's creation. The first duty, then, of genuine science is to decide whether this is a reasonable faith or an idle superstition; and if well founded, then to decide on the true meaning of the record in its scientific aspect, and the limits of the information it is really meant to convey. For in science, as in courts of law, the direct evidence of one trustworthy witness has usually far more weight than inferences, however plausible, which rest on doubtful assumptions, and various data all more or less uncertain. A series of maps and observations, by one competent eye-witness, of the geography of land and water ten and twenty thousand years ago, would do more, if it could possibly be had, to fix the chronology of quaternary or tertiary geological periods and changes, than the most subtle reasoning on observations of the last fifty years alone. Direct evidence, if only trustworthy, however limited in amount, outweighs a thousand ingenious guesses of the most learned men.

The Theory of Evolution completely fails to obey this first and simplest law of scientific induction. If its disciples had examined the claim of the Bible to be the word of God, fairly and openly, and then renounced it, openly and deliberately, as unsustained by real evidence, however we might regret their decision on high moral grounds, their course would be honest and consistent, viewed as men of science alone. But the course they have actually pursued, almost in every instance, is just the reverse. They assume the merely human character of the Bible, and by implication, the falsehood of Christianity, without attempting to prove it, almost as a self-evident truth. They dismiss the Bible by a side-wind, as if its statements were not worthy even of a passing notice; or mix it up, under the convenient phrase, "the cosmogony of the Hebrews," with the wildest dreams of heathen fable; and then cast the whole away, without further notice, as rubbish which does not deserve a moment's investigation from philosophers so enlightened and profound as themselves. Thus they treat the words of the living God, when they interfere with the free progress of their own speculations, with less respect than they would show to the depositions of an unlettered peasant on some meteor or aerolite which he had personally witnessed. But in so doing, they offend against the maxims of inductive philosophy, no less than against the lessons of Christian faith. They prove by their conduct that they prefer inferences to facts, and remote, conjectural conclusions and theories of their own from data most complicated and perplexing, to the fair and honest collection of all the evidence of every kind, and that reasonable preference of immediate testimony to skilful conjectures, which forms the very foundation of genuine science.

Christian believers, it is true, have often sinned by extreme rashness on the other side, and thrown a serious stumbling-block in the path of scientific men. Instead of a cautious and patient inquiry, how much or little the

Bible might be expected to teach on secondary matters, which do not form its main object, and what is its actual teaching, they have been too prone to palm their own ignorant prejudices or hasty impressions upon the sacred text, so as to drag it down from its true position, and turn it into a mere echo of the scientific ignorance and errors of each successive age. It is due, not only to science, but even to religious faith, that we should sift the testimony of Scripture with the utmost caution, where it touches on physics and cosmogony, and beware no less of overloading it with unfounded human glosses, than of casting it aside as mere Jewish legend. But no errors, however serious, of religious men, can ever justify men of science in reversing the first and simplest law of inductive research. There is a broad and a narrow way in the walks of science, no less than in Christian morals. The narrow way consists in the impartial acceptance, and careful weighing of all evidence, whatever its source or form may be. The broad way consists in rejecting direct evidence, when it seems to clash with our own theories, and choosing rather to develope freely our own hypotheses, by leaving out of sight well attested facts with which these disagree,

A second main principle of true induction consists in holding firmly by the most comprehensive lesson from the great body of evidence, and not reversing it in deference to partial anomalies or deviations, by which, at first sight, its reality may seem obscured.

Now the main question to be solved is the genesis of some twenty thousand species of vertebrate animals, co-existing with man, besides a far greater number, some suppose half a million, of insects and other lower forms of life, and perhaps half a million species of vegetables also. The general problem is to trace all these backward and upward, beyond the four thousand years of known history, in millions on millions of individuals, and hundreds and thousands of generations, until we can arrive at some reasonable view of their first origin. The one main inference from the experience of ages, confirmed by all modern science, in ten thousand species, and millions, perhaps billions, of individual men and animals, is that like produces like; and that with minor variations, derived from the parents, propagation is always of man from man, ape from ape, monkey from monkey, lion from lion, horse from horse, reptile from reptile, fish from fish, insect from insect, kind from kind. No single induction, in the whole range of science, is so firmly established, or rests on so vast an accumulation of experiences down from the earliest known period of human history. Each species; by this same law of wide and long experience, has a tendency to increase in numbers, unless restrained by the want of food, or the pressure of some more predatory race. So that the first lesson of a genuine induction, in mounting upward, is to recognize the sameness of the species as almost absolutely certain, but the number of each species as probably less and less, till it might be reduced either to a small number of pairs, or possibly even to a single pair.

This second principle of genuine induction, and the first in reference to the materials of science, points directly to the same view of the first origin of man and co-existent races, which meets us plainly in the Bible narrative. And it is this first and simplest lesson of actual induction, on the widest scale experience has ever supplied, which the Theory of Evolution reverses, and casts aside. In the backward ascent it substitutes another law wholly without evidence, for a law which is proved by millions and even billions of examples, without any proved and certain exception, through four thousand years; and offers a mere conjecture that, just beyond the limit of known history, the law of decreasing number within the same species was replaced by an opposite law, and by many abortive attempts to travel from one form of life to another, so that in the ascent the parents were more numerous than the offspring, but of a lower type and kind. It is hard to imagine how the inversion of the true laws of science could be more complete than in this substitution of a guess, which has no direct evidence whatever, for a grand fact, confirmed by millions on millions of examples in every past age of the history of the world.

The Theory of Evolution not only sets aside the most fundamental result of induction with regard to man and all existing species, but involves, when adopted, a kind of inverse miracle to that of creation, extending throughout the whole course of human history. Let us assume it, for the moment, to be true, that lower species have a power, in favourable conditions, to mount higher in the scale, and generate plants and animals of an order higher than their own. Let us go back six, or even ten, or twenty thousand years, to suit the hypothesis, to the time when man had actually appeared. The long and slow ascent had then been accomplished.

The Ascidian larva had climbed the steep ascent of the mountain side of being, and through the mouse or rat, or whatever lower form is preferred, had reached "the Simiadæ of the old world," and finally its human stage. Others had travelled upward, but with slower steps, and become weasels, mules, asses, horses, camels, lions, tigers, and all the variety of living things. But now, from six thousand years ago, the process is arrested, and as far back as observation can reach, no change from lower to higher species has been observed. No woman has given birth to a winged seraph, no ape or monkey to a human child, no lion to monkey or ape. A sudden frost has seized upon the grand life-impulse, to which such wondrous results are ascribed. It disappears wholly from view, and is seen no more. Ten thousand species, all inferior to man, live on with him side by side for thousands of years; and still, in thousands of millions of births, no single instance of this upward transition has been established. No single bear, by its efforts to catch fish, has been known to give birth to a cetaceous infant; and no rabbit, by the wish to escape from its pursuers, has bred a race of hares. Once admit the evolution theory, and a strange conclusion must follow. To escape from the Bible miracle, or the first origin of species by the word of God, we introduce a far stranger miracle of which the Bible says nothing. A gift or property, common to all the lower forms of life for myriads or millions of years, must have been suspended, by a perpetual negative miracle, during all the four thousand years of known history. The new hypothetical law, invented to dispense with the need of a Creator, turns all the known facts of physiology into one series of perpetual miracles on the largest scale. No marvel in Scripture can be so strange, or scientifically half so incredible, as this vast and ceaseless arrest, laid by an unseen Power on the action of a law, in ten thousand millions of cases, which must have been in ceaseless operation, by the theory, until the first dawn of human history for so many myriads of years. In its dislike of the miraculous, the hypothesis strains out a gnat, and swallows a camel. It dispenses with four days of miracles, affecting the first pairs of every living species, by creating a vast series of miraculous prohibitions of change, affecting all the later individuals of each kind for four thousand years.

The transition itself, when its supposed steps

are examined, will be found incredible, and almost impossible. Ten thousand species are held to have been evolved, the higher from the lower, and even man, through many intermediate links, from the larva of some old Ascidian. Let us consider the case of one species only, and a less violent change. Let the ass have given birth to the horse—a nobler species—at some remote period, and twenty steps have been required for the complete transition. A certain proportion, more favoured by circumstances, or more aspiring than their fellows, enlarged their size, shortened their ears, clothed themselves with a more flowing mane, and effected the first of twenty forced marches, the last of which was to land their future descendants in their land of promise, the attainment of a higher and nobler species. If the proportion were only one in a thousand, or in a hundred, or even in ten, then, supposing a million of asses in being, after two, or three, or six steps, the result would be reduced to a single pair of slightly transformed animals. No horse could have been procreated, for the change would stop short by the dying out of the new aristocracy, before progress more than half-way towards even a mule's position. We must suppose the change to extend to nearly one-half of the total number at each stage, or to be suspended, to give room for steps of increase in number alone, in order that a single pair of the nobler species might result after twenty similar transitions. To make the change even conceivable, all these conditions have therefore to be combined. First, the number of asses which desert their first type, and rise one-twentieth part above it, must be as great as the number which remain simply asses as before. Secondly, the self-transforming he-asses and she-asses must pair only with each other, and a law of caste and aristocratic preference be in strict and constant operation. Thirdly, the chance of regression, by every analogy, must have been as great as that of advance, and this would make it impossible to reach more than half-way on the upward ascent; and from a million asses a single mule would be the highest result attainable. Fourthly, since the law must be conceived to apply to the unchanged or less-changed animals no less than to the vanguard, the result would not be two species of equal number, but twenty species graduating from asses into horses, with their numbers nearly in geometrical proportion, from a million to one. Fifthly, since asses and horses now exist side by side, and have so existed for thousands of years, and the supposed change occupied at least twenty generations, the theory can provide no reason why asses should not go on climbing into horses, and horses declining into asses, so long as they both shall live.

To sum up the real conditions, we may present them in this definite form. If even so large a ratio as one in ten desert the unmixed type, and aim at a higher, and one-half of the offspring of such a pair inherit both the actual ascent, and the ambition to mount higher, the chance of rise in the next generation is only one in two hundred. Assuming a race of ten thousand millions of asses, the chance against the completion of twenty such changes by a perfect horse and mare would be a trillion of trillions to one. And this immense improbability, in the case of one species, must be multiplied into itself ten thousand times for ten thousand different species, to express the real likelihood of the evolution theory, even when its fundamental postulate is allowed. The ratio is immensely less than that of a mote or speck of dust compared with the whole extent of the starry universe.

The theory disagrees with the facts of geology, no less than with the constant, unbroken induction from the history of living species for six thousand years. Let us accept the uniformitarian hypothesis, and extend the geological changes in the way proposed by its advocates, over millions, and perhaps even billions, of years, and throw back the origin of man some fifty or hundred thousand years before historical time, and the place of Adam in the "Hebrew cosmogony." Indeed, long ages might well be needed for self-transforming "Simiadæ of the old world" to lose all traces of their bestial parentage, and assume the human face divine. When these vast admissions have been made to meet the wants of this new theory, what results will follow? The one semblance of a definite principle in the hypothesis so explained is, that the birth of a new species by natural selection and animal ambition is a slow and painful work, and that the period of its gestation usually exceeds, and greatly exceeds, the known extent of human history. The known species of vertebrates only are at least twenty thousand, while those of insects have been roughly estimated at half a million. The period of the slow and gradual development of this immense variety, by insensible evolution, must surely reach very far back, to the borders at least of the carboniferous age. On this view the fossil remains of all the secondary and tertiary formations ought to consist chiefly of a series of mean proportionals between existing species, the ten thousand thousand parent generations out of which they successively arose. Now the exact contrary is the truth. They consist of new types, most of them generically distinct from the actual Fauna, and almost all specifically distinct both from that Fauna and from each other. Instead of meeting the conditions of the theory, and bridging over the present intervals of species, they supply more than twenty thousand new species, to swell the vast number of types specifically distinct. Thus, Sir R. Murchison has remarked, "Beginning with the vertebrata, are not the fishes of the old red sandstone as distinct from those of the Carboniferous system, on the one hand, as from those of the Silurian on the other? M. Agassiz has pronounced that they are so. Are any of the crustaceans, so numerous and well defined throughout the Silurian rocks, found also in the Carboniferous strata? I venture to reply, not one. Are not the remarkable Cephalopodus mollusca, the Phragmoceras, and certain forms of Lituites, peculiar to the older Silurian? In regard to the corals, which are so abundant that they form large reefs, Mr. Lonsdale, who has assiduously compared multitudes of specimens from both systems, is of opinion that there is not more than one species common to the two epochs." Thus the hypothesis of evolution, with its necessary pendant of countless intermediary forms, is as flatly contradicted by the widest inductions of fossil physiology, as by the constant lessons of experience for four thousand years.

One crowning objection to the hypothesis of evolution, as an inductive theory, still remains. Its professed aim is to account for the genesis of all fossil and existing species, by regarding them as generated from each other. But its true and logical result is wholly different, to abolish species altogether, and replace specific types of life by a vast and immense range of individual diversity. All bounds and limits of species, on this view, must disappear. Life is a continuous function, like the successive phases of the earth in its orbit, from the polype to the lion, and from the ascidian up to man. Now the larger our knowledge of existing species, and the wider the range of time over which our discoveries extend, the more complete is the refutation, supplied alike by the present and the past, of such a theory. Let us compare each species to a small circle, the radius expressing the extreme limit of known variation. Few evolutionists will suppose, in most cases, that less than ten steps would suffice to secure an evolution of one known species into another. The world of vertebrate life as now existing, may thus, for our present purpose, be represented by twenty thousand small circles in one plane, at a mean distance from each other of ten times their own radius. Their collective area will thus be one hundred times less than the area of the plane over which they are spread. Now, by the theory, every circle has been reached by generations of life travelling towards it from some neighbouring circle; and since the structure and conditions of life are intermediate to the extremes, the numbers in these interposed stages, or the life density, must be supposed intermediate also. The chance that any particular form of life, any vertebrate animal, shall lie within these circles, and not in the wider area around them, is thus not more than one per cent. What, then, is the chance that all the known individuals of mankind, all known animals within the range of human experience, and all the fossils detected by geology, shall fall, as experience proves,

R

within these twenty thousand actual type-limits, and perhaps two thousand similar type-limits of vertebrate animals, which geology supplies? To estimate it rudely, we must take the whole number of individual specimens, living, or dead, or fossil, known to have been confined to these limits, which is not less than a hundred thousand millions for man alone, and for all the vertebrates must probably amount to a hundred billions, then double it, and append that number of ciphers to unity, and we have the denominator of the fraction which expresses the likelihood of the facts, as made known to us by the constant experience of long ages, on this new evolution theory. Its truth is thus mathematically impossible; unless we buttress it with a perpetual series of countless miracles, far more strange and unnatural than those Bible miracles, in the first creation of every species, which it strives to set aside, and thereby to dispense wholly with the Creator in the formation of the world.

## CHAPTER XI.

#### ON CREATION BY LAW.

An attempt has been made to reconcile modern theories of development with some acknowledgment of a Creator by the use of a new phrase, creation by law. There are many, who are impressed by the imposing claims of scientific evidence, set up on behalf of a continual evolution of new forms of life, and who are still reluctant to abandon wholly their faith, as Christians, in an All-wise Creator. Their syncretism embodies itself in this ambiguous term. The popular view, they urge, derogates from the Divine power and fore-knowledge. It represents the acts of creation as occasional, uncertain, capricious interferences with settled law. The Supreme Architect is reduced to the level of a human machinist, who needs to interfere, from time to time, to repair His own machine, or to introduce desirable changes in its complex machinery, of which He was unable to foresee the want when it was first made. Science, on the other hand, reveals more and more, in every part of nature, the reign of fixed and settled laws. Even those phenomena, which seemed once exceptional and capricious, like eclipses, and the combustion of explosive mixtures, are resolved, by larger experience or profounder thought, into regular results of the same abiding laws, under special conditions that are more rarely combined. Why should we not extend the same principle to the work of creation also? Why may we not believe that caprice and uncertainty have here no place, but that new creative acts result, in the wisdom of the Creator, by a kind of natural and necessary consequence, from a certain stage in the working of actual laws, and the previous state of the visible universe? Thus we may retain our faith in the existence of a Creator, and own His workmanship in all things; and still may escape from a superstitious encumbrance of the doctrine, and see Him working only by fixed laws of evolution, on which every stage of the world's history successively depends.

This general idea seems to admit of three varieties; first, that this creation by law is strictly continuous through all past history; secondly, that it is discontinuous, but periodic, the periods, like those of eclipses, depending on some special combination of physical conditions that have gone before; or thirdly, that creation properly was once for all, in the beginning, but of such a nature, that all later species of life and active powers were then bestowed in a latent form, so as to reveal themselves gradually in due season, and by an ascending scale of progress, without the need for any later and special interference of the Creator's hand. Each of these varieties will be found, I believe, on closer search, to involve a real and essential contradiction, so as to be, in the favourite phrase of some leading evolutionists, "literally unthinkable."

The first alternative makes creation by law a strictly continuous work through the whole course of past history. Now this simply denies Creation, and puts in its place a wholly distinct idea, that of a superintending Providence. What this Providence is to do is not explained, since the actual changes are referred wholly to pre-existing laws alone. But this constant presidency over all changes from moment to moment has no one character of a work of creation. It is a work of providence and conservation alone. Creation by law, on this view, is simply a fraudulent misnomer, to conceal the denial of creation altogether, and replace it by the presence of an idle Deity, like the gods of Epicurus, in all the changes of the universe; while their character is decided wholly by pre-existing laws, independent of His choice, will, and good pleasure.

The second alternative makes the creative acts periodic, and distinct from the hourly course of providence, but supposes them to be decided absolutely by the arrival, in due order, of some special combination of physical conditions. The great clock of the universe sounds the destined hour; and the Divine Workman steps in, at its bidding, obeys the call of the physical law, or combination of physical laws, and puts forth the energy which the hour imperatively demands. Lifeless, lonely, disconsolate Nature, in her distress, rubs her mysterious ring on some rugged azoic or palæozoic rock, and the Unknowable promptly replies—"What do you wish? I am ready to obey you as your slave, and bring the prescribed forms of life into being; I and all the other slaves of the ring."

Now this alternative assumes a wholly different character, according to opposite senses which this word, law, may be made to bear. If we use the word in its highest sense, for the great moral aims of God's universal providence, as discerned by the All-perfect Reason, God the Only Wise, then the statement is only the Christian doctrine, disguised under a phrase at once deceptive and ambiguous. No Christian believer admits that the acts of creation, which he assigns to the Most High, however incapable of being resolved into the effect of physical laws, are really capricious. He believes, on the contrary, that they proceed from that God, who is wonderful in counsel and excellent in wisdom; all whose ways are judgment, and who does nothing without a cause; who is wise, unspeakably wise, in all His ways, and holy, unspeakably holy, in all His works. "Concerning law," writes Hooker, "no less can be said, than that her seat is the bosom of God, and her voice the harmony of the world." Creation by *moral* law, or the wise plan and purpose of a Moral Governor of perfect goodness, the same who has determined for all men "the times before appointed, and the bounds of their habitation," is the constant faith and doctrine of the Church of Christ from the beginning. The reasons for its order, so far revealed either in Scripture or by science, are too deep and various for us to understand. But that the actings of the Creator are decided by no blind caprice, but by the highest wisdom, is one of the first letters in the alphabet of Christian Theology.

It is plain, however, that the phrase, creation by law, when used to combine the theory of development with the verbal acknowledgment of a Creator, must intend by the term physical laws alone. The reference is to no high moral purpose in the mind of a wise and intelligent Governor, but to some internal signal in the state of the universe, on which the creative action is conceived to depend. Now this involves a threefold contradiction. First, it confounds law, which is permanent, with a momentary, transient, phenomenal condition of the universe. For, by the present hypothesis, the acts of creation are periodic and discontinuous. Each takes place at some specific moment. Hence the determining cause cannot be laws of being, which are continuous in their action, but must be the momentary state alone. Not law, but a transient, momentary, evanescent result of the acting of many laws on innumerable atoms, is thus made the instrument by which the Creator calls into existence new beings. Next, it makes laws prescribed by the Creator already to existing things, the means or helps by which He creates things non-existent. But if creation by Divine

Power out of nothing is said to be unthinkable, how much more unthinkable must be a creation of new things by the limitations imposed on things which exist already! Physical law, in its very conception, like social law, implies control and limitation. Thirdly, the idea of a Creator of inscrutable greatness, compelled, without choice, to create at set times, either by laws already given to existing things, or by some transient, phenomenal result of those laws in a momentary condition of the earth, is equally absurd, frightful, and profane. It degrades the living God far below the level of the slaves of the ring and the lamp in Eastern fable. For the genie is supposed at least to serve the bidding of a human master. But this theory makes the ocean slime and mudbanks of some remote era impose their commands to create new forms of life on that Blessed and Only Potentate, before whom the highest seraphim veil their faces while they adore.

Creation by law is thus, in reality, a contradiction in terms. For the law must refer either to beings which already exist, to the new beings created, or to the great Creator. If to beings which already exist, it is self-evident that rules or laws prescribing the action of existent things, cannot call into being creatures which do not exist, unless we confound generation by a creative gift already bestowed with a new creation. In this sense of the phrase, generation by law is conceivable, but not creation. If the law refers to the newly-created being, this would imply that some property or properties of a being, when created, can be the cause of its creation, or can exist before the creature whose property they are. This is the same as to suppose that to-morrow can exist before to-day and be its cause. Or, thirdly, if the law be referred to the Creator Himself, the phrase will imply that some momentary state of the changing universe has a higher power than the Supreme Creator, and compels Him to put in exercise the mysterious power of creating new forms of life, by some fatal, unintelligible necessity. Such a view is no less unreasonable than profane.

Every act of creation must imply some law or limit of active power, assigned to the creature in the hour of its birth, by which its being is mainly defined, and on which all the acts by which its existence is recognized must depend. But this law is synchronous in time, while secondary in order of thought, with the being to which it belongs. As properties cannot possibly precede or cause the substance, whose properties they are, this law, imposed by the Creator, attends and cannot precede the gift of being. It is a result of the divine act, and cannot govern the act on which it wholly depends. It is true that, if acts of creation are successive, we may be sure that there is divine wisdom in the times when they occur, and a correspondence, which we may perhaps be able in some measure to discern, with the conditions of the earth, or other parts of the universe, when new forms of life are called into being. This is a creation by the wisdom of the Supreme Creator, who orders all things by number, weight, and measure, and comprehends the mountains in scales and the hills in a balance. There is a high and lofty sense in which the Most High God is a law unto Himself, and "the perfection which God is, giveth perfection to that He doeth." But in place of this solemn and glorious truth, the ambiguous phrase, "created by law," would obtrude on the unwary a degrading counterfeit, an eyeless Samson of prodigious strength, compelled by unknown laws of nature to grind in their prison-house, and from time to time to do surprising works of power at their bidding. How unlike is such a being to the God whom the Bible reveals to us, the Maker and the Judge of all, who speaks the word, and creatures start into being, and to whom that sublime apostrophe belongs, "Who hath known the mind of the Lord, or who hath been His counsellor? or who hath first given to Him? and it shall be recompensed to him again? For of Him and through Him and to Him are all things, to whom be glory for ever. Amen!"

## CONCLUSION.

THE doctrine of creation, revealed in the opening words of Scripture, agrees at once with the most certain conclusions of sound reason, that time and the universe had a beginning, and with the widest results of induction with regard to all the successive generations of plants and animals during the ages of known history. The progress forward, in every case, is not from like to unlike, but from the few to the many; and the only progress backward, which can claim really scientific evidence, is not from like to unlike, from the definite to the undefined, but from the many to the few.

The Theory of Evolution, on the other hand, in its momentary acceptance by so many hewers of wood and drawers of water for the building of the temple of science, and its wholesale substitution of ingenious guesswork for the evidence of facts, seems to hold exactly the same place in Physiology which the hypothesis of vortices held two centuries ago in Physical Astronomy. Each lays hold of a captivating analogy, and rears on it an immense superstructure, without submitting it to the test either of known facts, or of clear and intelligible reasoning. It was known that floating matter was carried round and round in a whirlpool. It was assumed that such a whirlpool of loose revolving matter did exist in the planetary spaces, and that the planets might in this way be carried in their orbits round the sun. The resemblance was close enough to fascinate the vulgar mind, and even to deceive the learned for one or two generations. But the defects were these. There was no proof that these whirlpools did exist. There was no attempt to prove that, in case of their existence, they would cause elliptic orbits. Nay, as soon as the excentric orbits of the comets were determined, they drove the ploughshare through the whole system. As soon as rigid tests were applied by Newton's cautious and exact reasonings, the hypothesis broke down at every point, and was shown to reverse nearly every real condition of the great and sublime problem of the starry motions. A true law was detected, and the shadows fled away, and the once favorite hypothesis is consigned to a limbo of forgotten vanities and plausible, unscientific dreams.

The Theory of Evolution, in like manner, lays hold of the partial variation, which outward circumstances or artificial breeding are known to produce within the same species, and erects it into a fundamental law, by which specific distinctions may be set aside, and the whole world of plants and animals may have grown, out of some obscure thing, called protoplasm, into the countless structures of this glorious universe. But all direct evidence of such variation is wanting. It is flatly opposed to the very largest and widest induction in the whole range of science. It starts from no clear conception of life, or of the nature of species, but from almost total obscurity and ignorance as to the very definition on which the whole theory depends. And when tested by the actual conditions of the problem, it may be shown, on almost every conceivable alternative to involve a mathematical impossibility.

To these fatal objections is added another, more decisive still to reverent minds. Its direct and plain tendency is to dethrone the Creator, and thrust Him far away from the thoughts of men. It sets before us nothing higher than the vision described by Milton as once witnessed from the open gates of hell:—

" The secrets of the hoary deep, a dark
 Illimitable ocean, without bound,
 Without dimension, where length, broadth, and
   height,
 And time and space, are lost ; where eldest Night,
 And Chaos, ancestors of nature, hold
 Eternal anarchy, amidst the noise
 Of endless wars, and by confusion stand."

The simple narrative of Scripture, which this theory sets aside with scorn, embodies and combines all the surest and grandest inductions of science, the constancy of species, their generative and multiplying power, and the ascending order and scale of being, from lifeless matter, through the plant, and lower animals, up to man, created in the image of God. And then it forms them all into the noble pedestal for a glorious series of Divine revelations; until we rise to share in the rest of the Creator, and in the worship of the spirits before the throne, when "the morning stars sang together, and all the Sons of God shouted for joy." As far as man excels the monkey, so far the blind guesses of irreligious science are excelled by the philosophical depth and simple and sublime grandeur of the very first page in the true and faithful sayings of the Living God.

www.ingramcontent.com/pod-product-compliance
Lightning Source LLC
Chambersburg PA
CBHW021356230426
43666CB00006B/547